PILOT TO PROFIT

What People are saying...

Clients

"I first met Lisa in 2009 as my special guest at a 'Women in Business' meeting I hosted in my community. It was there I was first introduced to social media as a business and political tool and where I learned of Lisa's ability to identify trends in the digital world. She was the owner of Parlez Wireless then but was embarking on a new project teaching others the value of social media.

Lisa has since moved on from her retail operations and into the consulting world where she has continued to help me and my team hone our social media relationships. I marvel at Lisa's command of emerging products and cutting-edge technology and I'm grateful for her advice over the years.

Now Lisa is sharing her successful business experience with all of us in her new book, *Pilot to Profit: Navigating Modern Entrepreneurship to Build Your Business Using Online Marketing, Social Media, Content Marketing and Sales.* Lisa walks us through building a solid business foundation, creating credible content, moving beyond our money mindsets, and harnessing social media to grow business. Lisa is successful because she sets clear goals, and in her new book she shows her readers how to emulate that success. You don't have to be a business owner to benefit from Lisa's advice, either. Learning about effective social media strategies can be helpful to those in commerce but also to those who are involved in community work as well."

—Lisa MacLeod, MPP

"I started working with Lisa to help me better understand social media and how to use it to grow my business. However, what I got was so much more! Lisa starts you from the bottom (the foundation) and works you up to the top (roof). She helped me gain clarity and focus around my money mindset. When I stepped out of fear...my business almost immediately started to become profitable. Lisa is amazing at helping you work with the whole business. From better understanding the numbers of your business to building your list, she gives you the knowledge you need to build a solid business. This book gives you everything you need to be successful entrepreneur!"

—**Elizabeth Fanslow**, The Fanslow Group

"*In Pilot to Profit: Navigating Modern Entrepreneurship to Build Your Business Using Online Marketing, Social Media, Content Marketing and Sales*, Lisa Larter, a proven, successful business coach and entrepreneur, simplifies what you need to know to ensure your business flourishes. She provides a clear blue print and methodology that includes positive insight, essential tools, and valuable guidance that only a person who has experienced success can do. If you are already in business or about to start a business, this book is a must read!"

—**Deborah MacDonald**, Entrepreneur, Investor, and Author

"Practice what you preach. Lisa's consulting business is a success story and I know that she personally follows the formula prescribed in *Pilot To Profit: Navigating Modern Entrepreneurship to Build Your Business Using Online Marketing, Social Media, Content Marketing and Sales.*

Lisa's book over-delivers in tactics and strategies to take your business to the next level of profitability and success. It reads just like you! I feel like you are coaching me, and that feels amazing because your words and wisdom come from a place of authenticity. Congratulations! I see your book transforming millions of entrepreneurs' lives."

—**Samantha Moonsammy**, Co-founder,
STARFISH creative events + inspiration inc.

"I have worked with many different coaches over the years, yet Lisa has proven to be one of a kind! One of Lisa's most precious qualities is that she makes a business owner know that she truly cares about your business. She doesn't just coach you. She actually helps you achieve concrete results. I truly believe that Lisa is gifted. She takes the time to walk you through the hurdles and has an intuitive sense in knowing exactly what you need in situations you may not know how to navigate. Recently, she gave me one single tip that when put into action resulted in the generation of 5 new clients. The results are clear. Lisa is the master of her domain and expects that you will do the homework she gives you. By following Lisa's advice, putting your business in order, and creating a plan, great things do happen! I refer to her lovingly as "Bossy Pants" and endorse her 100%."

—**Diane Valiquette**, Founder of the Separation/Divorce Resource Centre and Rebuilding Relationships Facilitator

"How does an increase of 36% in sales for the first two quarters of the year in an already lucrative business after beginning to work 1:1 with Lisa sound? Lisa's sincerity, business acumen, creativity, and wisdom are just some of the reasons why I so value having her in my corner. I'm so glad to call her my coach and my friend. Take the gems in this book to heart and mind—they really work if you make them your own. Congratulations on a very valuable contribution to the world of small business and entrepreneurs."

—**Wendy B. Rice, PsyD**, Licensed Psychologist, Rice Psychology Group

"Lisa Larter is a regular person and a self-taught entrepreneur. She is also committed to teaching the rest of the "regular people" in the world how to become financially independent and offers simple, but proven strategies to get there.

I met Lisa twice and watched her via Facebook for about 2 years before hiring her as my coach. She kept amazing me by posting things she planned to do and she would do them, no matter how big of a challenge they may be. She held herself accountable and made no excuses, she just got the work done. I knew I needed to work with someone and that was the kind of person I wanted to work with. So, I sent her a message and asked to speak with her.

Within 10 minutes of our telephone conversation, Lisa unravelled and revealed the mindset beliefs that I had around money, my worth, my ability to do well in the world, and to be paid for it! Lisa wasn't just a business coach for me. She has been my counsellor, mentor, and inspiration. Lisa's belief in me has helped me to create an entirely new person in my head… well, she was actually always there, however, Lisa helped me remove the veils and let her succeed.

I have been part of Lisa's Coaching program and Pilot Project programs. In 1 year, with Lisa's support and expertise, I have established a new website, a routine for generating content, developed a framework essential to my supporting those in grief, created program ideas, held my first intensive retreat on loss, written an eBook, and published a book, which is now available on Amazon! It's been a busy year, but truly the most productive year that I have had in my two-plus decades of being self-employed, and I have no hesitation in saying this is a direct result of my investment into Lisa's programs.

I am looking forward to the next year and seeing what magic I can make using the skills I have developed by working with this amazing woman."

—Janelle Breese Biagioni, RPC,
Author, Speaker, Grief Counsellor, & Educator

"I love Lisa's book. Bravo! It is so insightful and she breaks it down to be easily understood. Lisa comes from the heart in helping her clients. Lisa really knows how to teach and guide you to take on a project and turn it into gold. Thanks, Lisa, for sharing your experiences along the road and providing insight on how to do it better."

—Christine Norcross, Realtor—MBA, CRS, GRI, ePRO, ABR,
William Raveis Real Estate

"I loved reading *Pilot to Profit: Navigating Modern Entrepreneurship to Build Your Business Using Online Marketing, Social Media, Content Marketing and Sales* by Lisa Larter. The book is insightful, inspirational, authentic, and so real. I loved how relatable it was and I was able to see parts of myself into Lisa's story and most important, Lisa gives tips and strategies that support me in creating a profitable business, she brings a different perspective. Lisa has a way of sharing that inspires me to move with increased velocity towards my goals and reminds me of what is possible. It is clear and thought provoking and what I love is that Lisa cares enough to share herself and show me what it takes to make it in life in a way that is productive and authentic. This is an easy read and I encourage anyone that is striving to be successful to check out what this book has to offer."

—**Melissa Hughes**, Founder and CEO, Live Rich. Spread Wealth

"*Pilot to Profit: Navigating Modern Entrepreneurship to Build Your Business Using Online Marketing, Social Media, Content Marketing and Sales* by Lisa Larter tracks her journey from an indebted young woman who lived with a roommate to a highly successful, sought after internet entrepreneur. Following Lisa's blueprint can help you turn your business and financial life around with easy-to-follow steps illustrated with colorful and inspiring stories of Lisa's own journey. Get your highlighter, note pad, and a comfortable chair and start reading. You won't be able to put it down!"

—**Jack Cotton, CRS CRB**,
Luxury Real Estate Expert, Author, and Agent

"Since the moment I met Lisa and took her first program, my world of focusing on the business of my business has grown exponentially. Through her guidance and the structures she provides I have come to know what I did not know and needed to know to be in charge of and in control of my business. The depth of her gifts and talents in teaching the business of your business is incredible. Her programs offer rigor and substance along with providing the nuts and bolts, to the strategy, to the mental mindset, to the habits and practices of discipline for making your dreams a reality. At the same time she has your back championing you along the path as she stretches your comfort zone for the sake of your success.

Working with Lisa Larter is a game changer. I highly recommend her and her programs.

The book is going to be great and a gift to the entrepreneurs of the world."

—**Diana Gabriel, PCC**, Professional Certified Coach

"If you are a business owner who knows that it's time for your business to grow, that you are ready to reach more people, and you know it's time for you to have a greater impact on the people that you serve, this book is for you. Lisa Larter takes you through the process of understanding the key elements of a successful business from what she has learned from personal experience growing multiple successful businesses. Whether you are in retail, consulting, or have a brick-and-mortar business, Lisa will help you to apply what you can immediately do to improve and grow your business. Don't let another sale go by without learning from Lisa's experience. This book will make a profound difference in your business and in your life."

—**Pierrette Raymond**, Founding Franchise Partner of
1-800-GOT-JUNK?, Owner of Moving Forward Matters,
Professional Speaker, Author, and Educator

"*Pilot to Profit: Navigating Modern Entrepreneurship to Build Your Business Using Online Marketing, Social Media, Content Marketing and Sales* is filled with practical and applicable information to transform your business. Lisa shows how your business model, the content you create, and social media are integrally linked to gain more customers and drive increased results. She shows you exactly how to take a connection and turn it into a loyal customer. A must read for all business owners!"

—**Colleen Francis**, President and Founder of
Engage Selling Solutions, Author of Nonstop Sales Boom

Colleagues

"Lisa brilliantly lays out a structure to develop a business model that you'll love while also getting your message seen and heard by the right audience. She shares her proven methodology in this book to attract more leads and then shows you exactly how to convert them to clients. A must read!"

—**Melonie Dodaro**, CEO of Top Dog Social Media,
Author of The LinkedIn Code

"Straight talk on the truth about business, money, and what it really takes to make it. That's what you get when you read Lisa Larter's book, *Pilot to Profit: Navigating Modern Entrepreneurship to Build Your Business Using Online Marketing, Social Media, Content Marketing and Sales.*"

—**Alexis Neely**, Business Priestess &
New Economy Personal Finance Expert

"Congratulations! You will be so glad you decided to buy this book. I have known Lisa Larter for many years and can attest she is someone 'walking her talk.' Lisa is easily one of the smartest and savvy women I know. Sometimes when I get stuck on a problem I think, 'What would Lisa Larter do?' Why do I do that? Because the woman is tenacious, uses metrics like no one's business, and always does what is right for her clients. You will reap rewards a minimum of tenfold by buying this book. I cannot say enough good things about Lisa not only as a leader but in her ability to help you get to the next level."

—**Joyce Bone**, Honey Badger Extraordinaire

"This book is essentially a blueprint for small business owners who want to increase sales and profits in their business. Social media can be a huge distraction for business owners if they are not clear on exactly how to turn connections into customers. Lisa shows you how to use your content to build credibility, and then how to easily increase sales by being SWIIFT. Her SWIIFT model will change how you look at Social Media and Content Marketing."

—**Linda Clemons**, Sales and Body Language Expert

"As an entrepreneur, I often tell people that you go into business for one reason and one reason alone. You love what you do. However, it is easy to fall into the trap of being so busy working IN your business, you neglect to work ON your business. Lisa has strategically given steps not only to help you work ON your business, but how to work smarter, not harder through money tips, social media strategies, mindset techniques, and so many other top-notch strategies. Learn from the best. Lisa is a leader in anything business-related and in online strategies. Allow her experience to teach you how to continue to succeed and break through your ceiling. Now that indeed is smart!"

—**Kathy Smart**, North America's Gluten-Free Expert, Best Selling Author, TV Show Host, Dr. Oz Guest, Global News Community Health Contributor

"If you're ready for no-nonsense, street-wise, hard-hitting, how-to blueprint on building and running your business, Lisa Larter's got it for you right here, right now. Read this book. It will transform how you think, take action, and get real results in your business."

—**Christine Kane**, President & Founder, UPLEVEL YOU

"Unfortunately, as business owners today we face a huge challenge. The challenge of misinformation, half-truths, and downright lies when it comes to finding real information that helps our businesses grow… It's much like finding a needle in a haystack… and this is why most small businesses fail even before they get started… I've read many books, and most of them fall short of the complete picture of what it takes to start, run, operate, and make your business thrive… Starting, Running, Managing, Partnering, Mindset, Marketing, Measuring… Lisa has put together what I believe is a complete picture, for not only start-ups, but also businesses that want to go to the next level… Finally, you've found the needle… Thanks, Lisa, for putting such a great book together. I can feel the truth in every word…"

—**Stephan Stavrakis**—Positioning Strategist

"This book is a tremendous read for entrepreneurs and corporate executives alike. Having worked for Lisa a long time ago in my career, I can tell you her lessons have a lifelong effect in setting you up for success. It is tremendous to see her lessons shared as a leader in my past, coming to life in this book to impact more people eager to live better, happier, more successful lives.

Whether it is in regards of 'how you can vs. why you can't' or 'having a positive mindset vs. a negative mindset,' Lisa has 'walked this walk' in life and impacted so many like myself. I am so excited she is sharing these lessons with many more through this book. A 'must-read' for all those trying to grow their business, or start one. Pay special attention to 'Measuring What Matters,' very few know this better than Lisa Larter.

—**Marc Petitpas**, Vice President of Sales, Fusion Homes

"Finally, a book that makes sense and is full of quality content that can be used in everyday life. It is about changing your mindset and how you think about money. This book will enlighten you and reinforce your understanding of how to master the money game. This is a must read if you want to have financial freedom."

—**Judy O'Beirn**, Creator and Co-Author of *Unwavering Strength*

"Lisa Larter knows her stuff. She has grown her business into a world-class enterprise by developing and implementing the powerful strategies and practical tactics she shares in her book. I know they work because I've watched her apply them over and over. If you want to grow your business, buy this book. You can thank me later."

—**Michael J. Hughes**, NfR Consulting Group

"Heart-felt, wise, honest, and relevant. Lisa Larter shares her own personal journey from financial struggle to entrepreneurial success. As a small business owner, I find her inspirational advice demonstrates how even minor, gentle changes to our mindset can garner wonderfully impactful results."

—**Joyce Little**, JL Consulting, Inc.

"Lisa's unique genius shines through in her book as she tells the honest and vulnerable stories we can identify with—about money, fear, and other things that hold entrepreneurs back—and then hits you right between the eyes with the truth of EXACTLY what it takes to succeed. And, when I say exactly I mean specific, practical steps that leave you feeling like, 'Yes, I can do this!' Lisa's book is like having a business coach right at your shoulder, leaving no room for doubt about the action, mindset, and approach to take to succeed."

—**Cristi Cooke**, Creator of the Pillars of Genius™ Method

"A path to personal success and financial freedom are in front of us every day. Lisa uses her personal experiences to mentor small business entrepreneurs through the process in a practical manner. This read will leave you inspired and prepared to compete in our competitive marketplace."

—**Shaun Marshall**, GM Canada-Sales & Operations at Cohere Communications

"The boost you need to grow your business today! Through her transparent writing, Lisa shares her experiences and vast knowledge in a positive, clear way that will get you started, take you to the next level, or remind you what is important. A book for every entrepreneur!"

—**DeDe Galindo**, Granddaughter of Zig Ziglar, Realtor, Entrepreneur, and Speaker with the Ziglar Women

"In Lisa Larter's book, *Pilot to Profit: Navigating Modern Entrepreneurship to Build Your Business Using Online Marketing, Social Media, Content Marketing and Sales*, she shares what I call the 'real secrets of online success.' As one of the premier Queens of Social Media, she lays out the type of foundation you need to build for a profitable long-term online business, as well as show you through her stories and examples how to deal with all the issues that come up along the journey!"

—**Sheree Keys**, CEO of ShereeKeys.com and #1 Best-Selling Author

"Love this book! Lisa does an excellent job of walking the reader step-by-step through her proven system of building a profitable business in today's social world, based on quality relationship marketing principles. Social Media is the great amplifier; read this book to learn how to get your business in order so you can turn the right connections into your best customers!"

—**Mari Smith**, Author of *The New Relationship Marketing* and Co-Author of *Facebook Marketing: An Hour A Day*

Media and Speaking Organizations

"The title "business coach" doesn't even begin to sum up what we call the "Lisa Larter Effect." Lisa has the ability to bypass all of the minutia that can bog you down and zero in on a handful of key points that are the game changers. As new entrepreneurs with the women-centric SiriusXM radio show What She Said, we thought we had it down pat because the structure and the content of the show was 5-Star.

So initially, why didn't anybody know we existed? Enter Lisa Larter stage left and within a few sessions, we had begun to understand some of the deal-breaking mindset strategies involving content, social media, and more that would get us to the tipping point.

All we can say is thank you, Lisa, for your stellar business acumen and for setting us on the right path."

—**Christine Bentley, Kate Wheeler & Sharon Caddy**, Canada Talks—SiriusXM Channel 167

"Lisa Larter is quite simply one of the leading minds in business and marketing in our digital age. Her sensible advice on building a solid business foundation, developing great content, growing a strong social presence, and overcoming perceived obstacles is a must read for anyone who is, or ever will be, in business in the twenty-first century."

—**Paul Holmes**, Co-Producer, Social Media Camp—
Canada's Largest Social Media Conference

"Lisa Larter offers a life-line to entrepreneurs struggling break through personal and professional barriers to obtain their goals. Through personal experience, Lisa demonstrates how to turn the most daunting of challenges into stepping-stones on the pathway to success. With candor and humor, Lisa's direct approach cuts through the clutter of today's business world to offer clear, precise, and obtainable tools to make your dreams of today—tomorrow's reality. Mandatory reading for every business owner or those hoping to become one!"

—**Jeff Stamp**, National Television News Producer

"Lisa Larter and her unique entrepreneurial genius is my business benchmark and I have yet to meet a more gifted or more generous guru. As I grow my own business, I find myself constantly asking, 'What would Lisa do?' or 'What would Lisa think of this?' Her actionable wisdom has guided me in creating a solid revenue model, created expansion and opportunity—all while operating from my authentic self. If you find yourself caught in the eye of your own business storm, Lisa is the hand that lifts you up and out."

—**Shaun Proulx**, TV & Radio Personality,
Speaker, Author, and Publisher (ShaunProulx.com)

Corporate

"Lisa blends the best of both worlds. She leverages her corporate experience and delivers easy-to-use systems that positively impact bottom line results. Her approach is effective for both small business as well as corporations in navigating the often unclear world of social media."

—**Jackie Foo**, Vice President, Bell Corporate Stores

"Lisa makes reference in her book to a 'defining moment' in her life when after experiencing a windfall financial gain, resulting from the sale of the company she worked for to a larger company; she rethought the wisdom of the decision to build a dream home. As the head of Human Resources in Lisa's company, I witnessed how so many of her peers followed similar dreams with a noticeable increase of BMWs in the company parking lot! The decision by Lisa and her husband to sell the dream home and move to a 'fixer upper' was an important turning point in their lives. The wisdom of the teachings found in Lisa's book are based upon her real life experiences that have guided her to becoming a successful entrepreneur and business woman while enjoying financial freedom to live an enviable lifestyle. The real differentiator of Lisa's book, as compared to so many others offering advice on running one's business, is that Lisa's life journey is indisputable proof that her shared learnings, presented in a clear and simple manner, can generate profoundly positive results."

—**David Wells**, Retired Telecommunications Executive

"There are two things I love about this book. The honesty in which it is written, and the passion for the message behind it. It's a must read for anyone who is looking to break the financial woes cycle and be their own boss."

—**Helen Edwards**, Marketing Director, Lansdowne Place Mall

PILOT TO PROFIT

*Navigating Modern Entrepreneurship to
Build Your Business Using Online Marketing,
Social Media, Content Marketing and Sales*

LISA LARTER

New York

PILOT TO PROFIT

Navigating Modern Entrepreneurship to Build Your Business Using Online Marketing, Social Media, Content Marketing and Sales

© 2016 LISA LARTER.

Published in New York, New York, by Morgan James Publishing. Morgan James and The Entrepreneurial Publisher are trademarks of Morgan James, LLC.
www.MorganJamesPublishing.com

The Morgan James Speakers Group can bring authors to your live event. For more information or to book an event visit The Morgan James Speakers Group at
www.TheMorganJamesSpeakersGroup.com.

A free eBook edition is available with the purchase of this print book.

CLEARLY PRINT YOUR NAME ABOVE IN UPPER CASE

Instructions to claim your free eBook edition:
1. Download the BitLit app for Android or iOS
2. Write your name in **UPPER CASE** on the line
3. Use the BitLit app to submit a photo
4. Download your eBook to any device

ISBN 978-1-61448-845-3 paperback
ISBN 978-1-63047-576-5 eBook
Library of Congress Control Number:
2015905164

Cover Design by:
Rachel Lopez
www.r2cdesign.com

Interior Design by:
Bonnie Bushman
The Whole Caboodle Graphic Design

In an effort to support local communities and raise awareness and funds, Morgan James Publishing donates a percentage of all book sales for the life of each book to Habitat for Humanity Peninsula and Greater Williamsburg.

Get involved today, visit
www.MorganJamesBuilds.com

Habitat
for Humanity®
Peninsula and
Greater Williamsburg
Building Partner

DEDICATION

This book is dedicated to my husband, Paul St. Laurent. You mean everything to me. Thank you for your unwavering support and belief in me even when I don't believe in myself. I love you.

TABLE OF CONTENTS

What it looks like and how it feels when you start out. Starting a business can be messy, confusing, rewarding and fun. It's not the perfect story you may think it is.

Money is a funny thing. You start a business to earn more of it and then because of your beliefs you may find you do many things to repel the very act of earning a good living. Your mindset and your mindset around money is a key part of starting out.

Understanding what that means. A creative idea may work for a 12-year-old selling at the flea market, but you will need more than that if you want to pay your mortgage, employ other people, and travel the world. Your business model is the foundation for your success.

FOREWORD

By Peggy McColl

For more than 35 years, I have passionately studied personal and professional development and the steps needed to succeed both as an individual and business owner. I have trained with, researched, and studied the works of some of the greatest thought leaders to bless this planet.

However, the writings that have made the most significant impact on my life are incredibly simple.

You are holding an easy-to-understand, easy-to-apply book that is filled with profound ideas, strategies, stories, and truths. I know with certainty that when you study and apply what Lisa Larter is teaching, you will succeed far beyond your wildest dreams. Lisa knows what she is talking about, as her valuable expertise has contributed to the creation, growth, and success of many organizations. She talks the talk and walks the walk!

When Lisa told me that she was writing a book, I assumed that she was writing one on marketing … after all this is one of the many areas where she excels. However, if you think this is a marketing book, you need to think again. This manual provides valuable strategies and techniques for building a successful business, thriving in a highly competitive industry, and living a successful life.

What I love about Lisa's book is how she opens up and shares valuable lessons learned from her own personal experience. You will discover how she was completely broke, overwhelmed in debt, turned her life and business around by making much better decisions, and adjusting along the way.

The best thing you can do for yourself is to utilize this book as an in-depth guide for your life and business. Carry it with you. Study it every day. Put the ideas into practice. Share it with those you care about and with whom you want to succeed. Many years ago, a great mentor and friend taught me that if there is something you want for yourself, give it to another. Therefore, study, learn, and share Lisa's success strategies as much as possible. You will find that the benefits will return several fold. My wish for you is to be blessed with an abundance of success.

—**Peggy McColl**
New York Times Best Selling Author
www.PeggyMcColl.com

ACKNOWLEDGEMENTS

Gratitude is a significant part of my life. Therefore, I feel as if I could write an entire chapter recognizing the wonderful contributions of everyone who influenced this incredible journey, which began with an idea called The Pilot Project. Because of the phenomenal success of The Pilot Project, my first shout out is to my team of "Co-Pilots," the business owners and entrepreneurs who said an enthusiastic "yes" to taking that journey with me. Your feedback, support, encouragement, and belief continue to fuel my spirit every day. Thank you.

Peggy McColl, you were one of the first people to encourage me to write this book. Thank you for your support and for writing the Foreword. I will always look up to you and be grateful for your guidance, inspiration, mentorship, and friendship.

Chris Brogan, you challenged me to do more. Thank you for giving me candid feedback on my manuscript and for encouraging me to make the changes that would result in a better book. Your knowledge, expertise, and time are very much appreciated.

Thank you to Mia Redrick and her team for helping me with all aspects of this book, including introducing me to my publisher. Mia, if it weren't for you, this project would still be on my to-do list. Thank you for the gentle push every time (and there were many) I faced resistance.

Kathie Donavan, you have no idea what your inspiration meant to me towards the end. Your voice of reason and experience helped me to finish and to feel confident that my work was good enough.

To my team, especially to Shannon and Cassy, thank you for always having my back, for reading my work, and for letting me bounce my crazy ideas off of you even when those ideas were outside of working hours. I so appreciate you.

Last, and most important, thank you to my Mom. My positive and professional work ethic and values reflect the example you have shown me your entire life. I love you.

SECTION 1
PROFIT
PRINCIPLES

ACCIDENTAL
ENTREPRENEUR

"Use your life to serve the world, and you will find it also serves you."
— **Oprah Winfrey**

My parents separated when I was 4 years old, but it never occurred to me that my mom and I were poor until I was about 12. It was at this age that I started to notice the differences in what the other kids wore to school.

My clothes were purchased from Zellers, Kmart, and the local five and dime, and many of their outfits came from a boutique that sold higher-end designer clothes. One day, I asked my mom for a pair of designer jeans from that same store, and she told me that she could not afford them. She also informed me that I would have to get a job and make my own money if I wanted to buy jeans that cost that much.

Therefore, at the tender age of 12, I was hired and fired from a job within 24 hours. The position was located at a variety store in Haliburton, Ontario. The owners hired me because I was smart, personable, and hard working. However, I was fired because legally I was too young to be employed.

I was devastated but still determined to have those jeans. What I did next shocked my mom and showed her my determination. I gathered all of my old toys, books, and odds and ends from people in the neighbourhood and went to the local flea market. On my first day, I sold everything. I had made enough money to buy the jeans that I wanted and to buy a table to return the following weekend.

I became an accidental child entrepreneur. I made arts and crafts and chocolates and found a way to generate an income to buy the things that I wanted. In essence, I explored different methods to find out what worked. Then, at age 13, I was hired to work at the movie theatre and then the local five and dime.

Since 1983, I have sold to thousands of people, generated hundreds of millions of dollars in revenue for companies I worked for, coached hundreds—if not thousands—of people, and generated millions of dollars in sales in my own businesses. In addition, I have conducted several pilots inside of companies and businesses, always testing what works to make a company profit.

In 2006, I left the comfort of my corporate job and became a full-time entrepreneur. I have built and sold businesses, served amazing customers, employed tons of great people, and had the privilege of working with numerous business owners who wanted to learn what I know about building and sustaining a profitable business.

This book is what I know and believe it takes to start, build, and grow a business to keep profits in your pocket. It is my hope that it will serve as the blueprint to create or increase profits in your own business, as there are many moving parts that you must be aware of in today's world to build and sustain a profitable business.

Many entrepreneurs start because they have a creative idea but don't understand the mechanics of how a business operates. They have never created a business plan, never run a pilot or proof-of-concept, and never had to sell or network to grow their business.

They are like a homebuilder who tries to build a house with a hammer and no other tools. It's simply impossible to finish the project.

I have learned a thing or two about running a business, increasing sales, and making profits. In addition, I have found after working with many other business owners that my results not only speak for themselves, but are also above average. Many small business owners rarely hit the six- or seven-figure mark in sales and fewer women achieve this benchmark. In addition, a small percentage of women earn more than $100K a year. In essence, many small business owners struggle to pay themselves at all.

Many of the people I've coached or who have taken some of my online training programs aspire to create a modest living. This means they want to keep some of their profits and be reasonably remunerated for their efforts. However, they do not expect to become overnight millionaires. They just want to earn a good living, have the freedom of self-employment, and enjoy the things they desire in life.

I've worked with a lot of people over the years, some who have quadrupled their businesses by applying the principles I teach in *Pilot to Profit: Navigating Modern Entrepreneurship to Build Your Business Using Online Marketing, Social Media, Content Marketing and Sales* and even those who have attained their highest month or year in sales ever. Many clients have also used these strategies to close million-dollar deals, and a few have even doubled the size of their businesses and acquired new ones along the way.

Why only some? Why not all? Because the ones who experienced the exceptional results realized something that many overlook. There is a tremendous amount of good information provided in this book, but information *alone* is not enough.

These people have experienced success because they applied the concepts and kept making an effort even when it was challenging. Their commitment to achieving more in their life and business has allowed them to reach higher levels of success than they believed or even imagined possible.

That is the most rewarding work I can do—making a difference in the life of someone who has risked everything to be an entrepreneur.

This book is not full of hype; however, it is filled with proven, tested methods that have increased profits for others. These methods have worked for home-based businesses, shopping centers, retailers, authors, speakers, consultants, and even individuals in network marketing organizations. These methods have been tried, tested, proven to work, and have garnered excellent results.

What should you expect to gain from your investment of time in reading or listening to "Pilot to Profit"? This is what I promise to share with you:

1. The creative process of starting a business. What it looks like and how it feels. Starting a business can be messy, confusing, but also rewarding and fun. It's not the perfect story you may think it is. It's hard to make a profit at first, but it is not impossible.

2. Your mindset and your mindset about money. Money is a funny thing. You start a business to earn more of it and then because of your beliefs may find yourself doing many unexpected things to repel the very act of earning a good living. Your mindset and your mindset around money are key parts of building a business.

3. Defining your business model and understanding what that means. A creative idea may work for a 12-year-old who wants to buy a pair of jeans. However, you will need more than that if you want to pay your mortgage, employ other people and travel the world. Your business model is the foundation for your success in business.

4. How to measure what really matters in your business. It's only a business if you're making a profit. Therefore, your ability to really understand key business metrics is critical if you want to create long-term and sustainable results.

5. Your content is your credibility when your customer is looking for you online. In today's world, what you write is relevant and if you don't write it online, you pretty much don't exist. It's the way people find you and judge whether they want to do business with you. It's your calling card and the first impression that your business makes on others.

6. The beauty of email marketing and how simple emails can make your cash register ring. When you communicate effectively via email, you can build a solid community and create compelling offers that move your customers to buy.

7. The secret to selling on social media. Most people get this all mixed up. They apply spray-and-pray tactics and wonder why social media doesn't work. This chapter is the formula I use to get real and measurable results from social media.

8. Relationship marketing: what it means and how it can help you know and reach more of your ideal customers. Learn my SWIIFT method and stand out from all of those other marketers who are just looking at "What's in it for me."

9. Demystify social networks so that you know which ones to use and why. It is a myth that you have to be on and use every social network daily. Likes on Facebook don't pay your

mortgage; however, when you figure out which networks allow your business to turn connections into customers, you are on your way to increasing sales and profits.

10. How to sell. What's the point of having people interested in your business if the moment they are in front of you, no one can close the deal? Selling is not a bad thing. You can serve and sell in a way that feels good and adds value for others. You'll stop shirking sales and start embracing the skill. No one will ever sell your business like you do.

11. What to do when you finish this book. Like I said earlier, the application of the methods is going to help you achieve results. If you feel like this book is exactly what you have been looking for to take your business to the next level, I will share with you other ways that you can take action and grow your business.

If building a business were easy, everyone would do it! However, it takes courage, conviction, confidence and a whole lot of hard work to build a successful business and I believe you can do it.

I dropped out of high school during my last year. Although I was so close to completing my studies, I never finished. I used to live with my bank account in a state of constant overdraft, which is even worse than living pay check to pay check. I also don't have a post-secondary education and none of my family was entrepreneurial. I most certainly never received a hand out or was given a silver spoon or a trust fund.

Today, my life is amazing, and I owe this solely to the action I have taken to achieve my ideas and dreams. I have tested many things, examined my failures and challenges, and found ways to go over, under or around the obstacles in my path. You will definitely benefit from all of that experience in this book.

You are the same as I am. In fact, you may be more educated, have a more supportive family, and even have more financial resources than I started out with. The question is: Are you ready to be the leader of your own destiny?

I believe that you are...I also think that you are reading this book for a reason.

CHAPTER ONE

THE FIRST SALE IS ALWAYS TO YOURSELF

"Nothing is impossible. The word itself says 'I'm Possible.'"
– Audrey Hepburn

When I worked in the corporate world, anytime we had an idea we would run a pilot to test it. We needed a proof-of-concept or a trial to validate if the idea was a good one before we would decide whether to roll it out to the entire company. That is always the objective of a pilot.

As a young manager working in clothing retail, I used to run pilots inside of my store before I even knew what they were called. I was what they called a "Fire Fighter," which is the type of manager sent to underperforming stores to clean up their processes, inspire the team, and turn around sales.

In one store where I worked, everyone believed it was a professional market, which meant that we sold suits. However, I had a theory that might not be completely true, and so I conducted a test at the front of the store by merchandising some cool, trend-setting baby tees and sundresses.

I put together a cute display that mimicked the style I had seen on the popular TV show "90210," and the next thing I knew those dresses and baby tees were selling like hot cakes! All of a sudden, the store that was known for selling suits was a trend-setting location. The president of the company called me because she wanted to know what was going on since those two items were NOT selling anywhere else.

I had done something I wasn't supposed to do when I merchandised those dresses at the front of the store. I took an idea and I acted on it. I was driven by results in my store and I had a hunch that this would work. Therefore, I tried it and the next thing I knew, my idea and results had a tremendous impact on the entire company because shortly after my call with the president, everyone was being told to merchandise those dresses and baby tees the way I had and they were all getting similar results.

You have ideas, too. You may have an idea for a brand-new type of business and ideas to make your existing business grow. When you are entrepreneurial, you have creative ideas all the time.

The challenge, however, is turning those creative ideas into concepts that work.

That's what this book is about. It's my blueprint on what you need today to build a successful and profitable business because you need more than just a creative idea. I will share each of the concepts I have piloted in my own business, used with other business owners, and watched generate profits repeatedly.

When you pilot something in your business, you want to create, test, evaluate, fix, and then test again. It's a whole lot of trial and error to determine what works and what does not. In this case, I've done the testing for you.

Now it's time for you to take your idea and do the same. First, you have to convince yourself that your idea is worth it.

The First Sale Is Always To Yourself

You have to convince yourself first that the vision you have for your business has legs. You need to sell yourself on your own business ideas if you are ever going to be successful with selling it to others. Selling is really your ability to transfer belief, and the first person you need to convince is you.

Believe that you are capable of building this business and in selling your idea to others. Believe that your product or service is of value and is worth buying. You're going to have to be able to sell this belief to YOU first; otherwise, you won't be successful selling to others.

Martha Stewart started out making pies in her kitchen and selling them at the farmers market. She was not the Martha Stewart back then that she is today. She started her business the same way as you and I—as a little idea that she tested and refined, which then grew into something much bigger.

Her first pilot was selling pies at the market. Look at her now and the profits in her business.

Martha Stewart had to go through three phases in her business: 1) Start Up, 2) Growth Mode, and eventually 3) Scaling to get where she is today. I am sure her ideas in the very beginning did not include everything her empire is today, however, it did start with a belief in her own ability.

You and your business can get stuck in start-up mode for an exceedingly long time if you do not have belief in both yourself and in your vision.

Belief in Yourself

If you can't sell belief in your ideas to yourself, you won't be able to sell it to someone else. You must have unwavering belief in your vision for your business. Therefore, you must look at the details that go into your business as your vision crystallizes for it to become your reality.

My First Business Pilot

My first vision for a business was far from grand. However, it was more of a test to see if I could actually do it. I had an idea for an organic basket business back when selling organic products was not a popular concept.

I conducted a great deal of research online, found suppliers and products that I could use, and started by spending lots of my own money making organic gift baskets to give away to friends and family members. Yes, *give away*. I was spending more than I was making when I first started that business.

One day, a homebuilder contacted me who wanted to buy gifts for his customers after they bought and moved into their new home. This one customer helped me to build my own confidence in my product, allowed me to grow, and expand my business from an idea that was costing me money to become a company that made $30,000 a year in sales "on the side" while I worked my full-time job.

My ability to take that vision and create a business that generated an income allowed me to build enough confidence to eventually quit my job and open my first retail store, Parlez Wireless, an authorized TELUS Dealership, in 2006. I was confident that if I could generate $30,000 a year in sales working one weekend a month, I could do much more if my focus was full time.

My vision back then wasn't just about creating gift baskets. My vision was about living a freedom lifestyle. I just didn't know how to get there.

I aspired to be self-employed and to create as much success as possible in my life through my own actions. I dreamed of a life of freedom where I was financially secure, could travel as much as I wanted, and work from anywhere. I am guessing you can relate to that desire, too, if you are reading this book.

The Organic Basket Company was my first pilot, the building block that allowed me to create and strengthen belief in myself. I made many mistakes, learned numerous lessons, and kept trying because I knew there was more to accomplish if I kept trying. Since that time, I have built multiple six- and seven-figure businesses. Today, my business can operate from anywhere in the world and I have a team of people who serve and support our customer base.

My basket business was my starter business. It was the first step in building my confidence so that I could take on a much bigger vision and bring it to fruition. Your first business may or may not be your last. If you are like me, you will learn many lessons from that first business that you will apply as you continue on the path of entrepreneurship. Pay attention to the lessons you learn from everything that you try, and reinvest both the learning from your mistakes and the knowledge you gain along the way back into your business.

The creative process of building a business is never as clean or as easy as one expects. You will be challenged in numerous ways, as there will be decisions that you regret and some things will be far easier than you ever expected. Pay attention along the way.

At the risk of sounding "woo woo," listen to your gut. If what you are doing makes you feel "icky" inside as if you have a heavy piece of concrete in your gut, you may not be on the right path. Learn to listen and trust your instincts along the way, let go of the things that don't feel good, and embrace the things you love so much you would almost do it for free.

Be Careful Who You Take Advice From

Don't take business advice from individuals who have never successfully run a business. Your friends and family may not have what it takes to start and build a business. In addition, don't let their opinions stop you from trying. If I had listened to those people who thought I should be grateful to have my corporate job, I wouldn't have accomplished what I have and most certainly wouldn't be writing this book.

The key lesson here is observe, assess, and redirect. Pay attention to your vision. Nurture it, feed it, and explore what you need to get it off the ground. Be kind to yourself. Building a business takes time, effort, many trials, and many resources.

You live in an amazing time, where many have gone before you. Therefore, you can learn from those experiences and fast track your own progress.

Chapter Two

Your Money Mindset

"When you change the way you look at things,
the things you look at change."
– Wayne Dyer

oney is a funny thing. It's an emotional roller coaster and one you want to gain control of in your business.

Business Is an Exchange of Money for a Product or Service

Most people go into business to do something they're passionate about. Many talk about the difference between being an entrepreneur versus a heart-centered entrepreneur, as though doing the right thing is more important than making money. In business, it's kind of like saying, "If you're an artist, you have to be a starving artist."

This is a false belief.

You can be a good, caring business owner and still make money. The important thing is for you to be okay with your worth and your value. When you *really* understand that business is an exchange of money for a product or a service, you begin to be okay with receiving money—for the product, service, or value that you are offering.

If you're struggling with that concept, trust me, you're not alone. It's something that everyone struggles with, including me from time to time.

Recently, someone set up two different Facebook profiles and a Facebook page for her business. She was concerned about which profile to keep and how to delete the page so that she didn't lose the information that she wanted to keep. She sent me a couple of questions on Facebook and I provided her with assistance.

Later that day, she sent a thank you email and an e-transfer for some money as payment for the help that I had provided. However, I struggled with accepting the payment, even though a part of me knew that she wanted to pay for services rendered and I should just accept the money. I accepted her payment, but it was something I had to wrap my head around because I had not asked her to pay for my help.

You will face similar situations and struggle in this same fashion if you are a generous person and even more so if you own a service-based business where your revenue-generating asset is your time and knowledge.

So, what is the value of your time and expertise?

After a 15-minute conversation, someone who worked with me turned one idea into an extra $15,000 that year. If someone makes an extra $15,000 after just 15 minutes, does that mean the value of my time is worth $60,000 an hour?

That may seem a little extreme, but if business is an exchange of money for a product or service and I have provided that service, what is the value of my time? What would you pay if someone could show you how to make $15,000 in 15 minutes? Would you pay $500? $1,000? $1,500?

You might feel like it was just 15 minutes of your time… however, the outcome or the value was huge for the other person. Start paying attention to the outcome your business provides others.

When it comes to money, your mind will play tricks on you. Learn to be okay with making and receiving money. There will be times when you think you are undeserving, it was too easy, etc., and feel funny about accepting payment. Contrary to what you may have been taught as a child, money is not the root of all evil. You will need to challenge the beliefs you may have that people with money are bad or don't take care of others, because those beliefs may be getting in the way of your own success.

Always remind yourself that business is an exchange of money for a product or service. This is your business, it is not a hobby, and it is not a charity or volunteerism.

When I was 12 and set up shop at the flea market, I was too young and naïve to even consider that I shouldn't take people's money when they bought items from me. This circumstance made a significant difference to my money mindset. I learned that I could independently make money and, even more important, that it was okay for me to do so.

From a young age, I always found ways to make money; however, that's not to say that I didn't struggle with the money that I made.

I've Been Broke and It's Not Fun

There was a time in my life when things were really bad.

It was 1994. I stood in the kitchen of the apartment I shared with my roommate looking at the caller ID as the phone rang and rang, knowing that it was the phone company. I was holding the final notice in my hand, which said that they would disconnect the line if the bill wasn't paid right away.

I wouldn't get paid until Friday, and my checking account was already in overdraft. I let the call go to voicemail because I knew what they wanted, and I didn't feel like going through the humiliation of telling them that I couldn't pay my bills.

In 1994, that was the story of my life. My account was always in overdraft, my credit card always carried a balance, and my bills were paid, but always late. I had a loan with the bank from reconciling debt that I had re-reconciled every year for the past 3 years. And, I owed my dad money plus interest for bailing me out.

Financially, I was a disaster. I had a full-time job as a retail store manager and was making what was considered decent money back then.

The problem was that I was spending more than I had, and spending frivolously. I wish I could say that my debt was the result of investing in something of value. But, truthfully, the money went to hair, makeup, clothes, and entertainment.

It was superficial and essentially worth nothing. My mindset and belief in myself were way out of whack.

I thought how I looked mattered more than who I was.

Henry Ford said, "Whether you think you can, or you think you can't— you're right."

My belief in myself was at an all-time low, and I was overcompensating for my lack of confidence in myself by spending money I didn't have.

If you understand that feeling or if you are in that situation, I want you to know that fixing your money mindset is the first step to getting yourself on track and in building a successful business.

Your mindset around money could be sabotaging your profits right now and you don't even know it.

Being Okay with Receiving Money

To be okay with receiving money you must examine your beliefs about money. If you're not clear about money, you'll go round in circles. When I'm clear on money and what I need it for, good things start to happen for me. I become very clear on exactly what I need to do, too.

When I quit my safe and secure corporate job and opened my retail store, it was scary because I walked away from a great income, job stability, benefits, and stock options. Even though it was scary, it was also safe because I left my job to do something I knew how to do well. It wasn't as risky as it could have been, and turned out not to be as challenging either.

About 2 years later, I remember being at our cottage in Nova Scotia and telling my husband that I wanted to set up another business, generate $250,000 per year in sales, and spend our winters somewhere warm and sunny. I was super passionate and jazzed about this new idea. I think he thought I was crazy at the time, but what happened over the next 5 years was exactly that. We sold the retail store, my second business far exceeded those initial numbers, and we bought a second home in Florida.

In the first business, I chose the safety of doing something I knew I could do. In the second business, I was clear on what I wanted to achieve and the value I was prepared to give to others from the beginning. I felt confident in my value, even though, as you will see shortly, I still needed to do a bit of work in that area.

It all came down to my money mindset. Think of your money mindset as a muscle. It doesn't matter what your money number is. The important part is to set goals for yourself and to be clear so that you are okay to receive this money.

It's like working out in the gym. When you go to the gym and start lifting weights for the first time, you can only lift a small amount. However, if you lift weights every day, over time you'll become stronger and be able to life much heavier amounts. You don't go in expecting to lift the heaviest weight because you know that you can't. It's the same with money. What you charge needs to be in alignment with the actual value of the product or service you offer or it will feel out of alignment.

Your money mindset is developed in the same way. Start with something small and watch your confidence grow. Maybe for you, it's charging $100 per hour or earning $1000 per week. The number doesn't matter. The goal and working towards it is what strengthens that muscle. Entrepreneurship is a marathon, not a sprint.

For me, the most powerful thing you can ask yourself is, "How can I?" versus thinking, "I can't." When I hear that someone is paying himself or herself $20,000 per month or when I hear that someone is paying himself/herself $10,000 per week, I think, "How can I do that?" My thoughts are always inspired by what others have done, and I choose not to think that those things are not possible for me. I believe if it is possible for him or her, then it is also possible for me. And that means it is also possible for you.

That's how your thoughts can strengthen your money mindset. Be open to the possibility, and challenge your mind to show you the way to what you want. It might sound old-fashioned, but some of my best ideas feel like they have been a gift from someplace larger than me. Your mind is powerful, more powerful than you can imagine.

NEVER think, "I can't do that," because that's a self-defeating thought. Always think in terms of "How can I?", and make it a fun experiment of exploring exactly how you can make all you desire in your life and business true for you.

In order to strengthen your money mindset muscle, the most important thing you can teach yourself is to learn how to generate additional income. That is my challenge to you as you read this chapter: explore and consider how to achieve this goal.

Be open, be curious, find a way to make an extra $100 today, and look at what you did to make it happen. It doesn't matter if you sell something you own to a consignment store or sell a program online. It's the act of making it happen that shows you and your mind that you are capable of generating income if you really want it.

If you want to make $200 a week more, set that as your target. If you want to make $1000 a month, start with $100 a month and work your way up. Train yourself to attain small goals and then keep gradually increasing the goal as your confidence and skill grow. Once you know how to make an extra $100 a month, stretch yourself to make $200 a month, then $500 a month, and so on until you reach $1,000.

When you start making deals with your mind about money, your money muscle gets stronger and you start to play in a bigger space. When you have done it once, you know that whatever you do, it can be done over and over again. Not only can you do it again, you can do it bigger and bolder, adding another zero and another zero.

However, it starts with that very first goal!

My first goal was the $100 I needed to buy those jeans—after that I made another $100 because I wanted another pair! Prove to yourself that you can conquer your limiting money beliefs one step at a time, as it will be the confidence builder you need to build and grow your business.

So, go ahead and set your financial goal, and then figure out how you are going to make the money you want. Don't forget to include a reward for your efforts along the way too!

In 2012, on a flight home from a conference I was feeling really inspired and began to think about how I could make $1 million in my business. I sketched out what a million-dollar plan for my business would look like. The simple act of sketching out what it would be like to own a million-dollar business started to move me in that direction.

When I first sketched it out, I was nowhere close to $1 million a year. In fact, I had just hit the six-figure mark. However, less than 12 months after writing out that plan, my business was more than half way there. That's the power of your mind when you explore what is possible for you.

Don't be afraid to look at your numbers. Understand that your mindset affects not only the money you make, but also the money you keep! Remember, earlier in my life I had a good job but I spent more than I made, putting my bank account in overdraft!

You can make $1 million a year, but if you spend $1 million and $2 dollars, you are worse off than someone who makes $20,000 per year and spends $15,000.

It's not only about the money you make. It's how you treat and keep that money, too.

Many people are too concerned with what other people think. They spend money on appearances and things that aren't really important and they over-extend themselves on credit, all because they are worried about what others think.

People today carry more debt than ever before in history. You don't have to live that way. You don't have to spend money on things you don't need. If you can't afford something, then don't buy it until you can. It's that simple.

When you start to make money, you don't have to spend it all. It's okay to keep some. You don't have to go out and buy a mansion that eats up all of your income. Maybe you can afford the mortgage payments, but you can't have nice furniture because you've literally maxed out on all the money you have. Therefore you have no leverage because you are spending everything!

When you start to make more money, respect the extra money you make and keep some of it.

The accumulation of that money gives you power and freedom. Eventually, when you have enough money, you can invest it in different things that will earn you more income, too.

Rich people know that money helps you make more money and that you need to hold on to some of your money and invest wisely. This is a key part of overcoming your money mindset.

Many people impose limiting beliefs on themselves when it comes to money. You may compare yourself and your business to what the industry charges or to someone else's success that is further down the path and feel that you aren't as good.

The problem with that is that you can't see the uniqueness of your own path when comparing it with someone else's path. Comparison always breeds misery.

Earlier in this chapter, I described a situation that I put myself in financially.

How did I go from that pattern of living in debt to the life I have today?

The truth is that my priorities changed, and consequently, so did my behaviour. In 1995, I started dating the man who would become my husband. Later that year, when we decided to live together, he told me he did not want to rent an apartment; he wanted to buy a house. I had looked at houses before, but the down payment was completely out of reach for me. There was so much debt in my life that I couldn't catch up, much less save.

With a good job and another part-time job on the side, my husband was making more than double my income. He had saved some money and had enough for us to put a small down payment on a house. This was scary for me because I had always been bad with money. I grew up in a very poor family, and all I knew was how to struggle when it came to money.

I needed to make some choices about my life and my behaviour with money if this was going to work. When you change the way you do things, you change the outcomes in your life. I made some choices that were more responsible, which made a big difference in my life.

First, we made some sacrifices. We moved in with my husband's mom for 6 months so that we could save money for our new home. This was a sacrifice that set us up for success.

Second, we bought second-hand furniture when we moved in so that it would not cost as much to furnish the house.

We didn't pay for anything on credit cards and we didn't eat out at restaurants. In fact, we ate canned and frozen prepared meals because it kept the cost of the groceries low.

About 1 year after we moved into our house, I was recruited to work for a new company and I did something completely out of the norm: I asked for more money when they offered me the job. Before my first paycheck arrived, I went to the bank and instructed the bank to redirect all of the extra funds towards paying off my debt. By doing so, I paid off my debt 2 years ahead of schedule.

The old me wouldn't have done that.

Why did I share that with you? My journey from being broke and financially irresponsible to where I am today is part of my own money mindset lesson.

You can only change your money mindset and the way you currently do things if you want to. How you think and what you believe make a difference. The reason for you to change has to be greater than the reason for staying the same. You must have clarity on why you want to change your relationship with money if things are to change.

Our home, the opportunity my husband gave me, and proving to myself that I could do this was enough for me to change both my mindset and my behaviour. Sometimes it takes someone else believing in you, in order for you to also believe in yourself.

Feast or Famine in Your Money Mindset

When you lack security and confidence over who you are and what you have, you will always try to prove to the outside world that you're bigger than you really are.

If you have $100 and you spend $120, you are in the hole. When you spend more money than you make, for whatever reason, you will always try to play catch-up.

At some point, you will be facing bankruptcy because you never do catch up and if you do, it is likely that you will extend yourself again unless you change your money mindset.

Until this changes, you will always be stressed out when it comes to money.

If you stop worrying about what other people think of you, chances are you will spend money responsibly versus living to impress others. I say this from my own personal experience. In my 20s, I bought all of the best clothes, went out to the clubs all the time, was the social girl at the bar buying drinks for everyone else. In the meantime, I couldn't pay my telephone bill!

Your story might not be the exact same as mine, but I have a feeling we are the same at the core.

Today, my husband and I own three homes. We don't live in a big, fancy house because we made the decision not to be excessive in our spending.

We have a modest home in Naples, Florida, a cottage in Nova Scotia, and we have just built our third home, a beautiful an ocean front property in Nova Scotia.

My internal need to impress others no longer exists; otherwise, I might still have the desire to acquire and the disease to please. When you let go of the need to impress others, yours will be too.

Set your goal and work towards it by considering four key areas that will enable you to challenge and overcome the limiting beliefs of your money mindset.

Four Key Areas to Improve Your Money Mindset

There are four key areas that I believe impact your mindset and, ultimately, your ability to achieve success in life and to obtain financial freedom:

1. Clarity
2. Belief
3. Fear
4. Self-Discipline

Clarity

The first step to getting what you want in life is knowing what it is. This includes money.

In the book *The Path of Least Resistance*, Robert Fritz speaks about current reality and desired state.

Let's try an exercise now to illustrate what this means.

I want you to imagine an elastic band that you have stretched vertically between both your hands until it is tight. The top of the elastic band represents the desired state that you want. The bottom of the elastic band represents your current reality. The band is tight, strained, and uncomfortable, almost ready to break. Fritz refers to this as structural tension. There are only two ways to remove the tension that exists between what you desire and your current reality.

You can either lower your vision for your desired state, or you can start to move closer (take action) towards your desired state from your current reality. This simple metaphor is powerful.

My question for you is this: Is your elastic band taut with tension or is it not being stretched at all?

That elastic band represents your life and business. Do you want both to be really great or do you want to just exist? There is a difference between living and being alive. There is a difference between letting life happen to you and creating a life you desire. The most successful people I know take *full ownership* of where they are in their life and know that their actions brought them to where they are today.

Oprah Winfrey says, "*Luck is when preparation meets opportunity.*"

The first part of the equation is knowing exactly what you want. You can't be prepared, or even see the opportunity, if you don't know what you want. The other powerful part of clarity is knowing your *why*. Saying, "*I want to have a million dollars in the bank,*" isn't enough.

You need to know exactly what you want and have a compelling why. It also helps when you know a bit about *how* you will get there. For example, when I started my consulting business, I set some very clear goals:

1. Create a business where I can work from anywhere.
2. Work with people from all over the world and teach them what I know about business so they can be more successful.
3. Generate $250,000 a year in sales.
4. Live by the ocean, spend my summers in Nova Scotia, and my winters some place warm and sunny.
5. Make my husband proud of my accomplishments and prove to myself that I can do this.

When I set these goals, we were at our cottage in Nova Scotia and still owned our retail store. When I told my husband, he said, "*That's great. What about the store? Do you think you could start to pay yourself there first?*" I had been running the store for 2 years and had not paid myself any income yet. He wasn't being mean, he was encouraging me to reap the profits that I had been making, and it was time.

That was the fall of 2008. In January 2009, I started to pay myself at the store, and by the end of 2012, I had accomplished all of those goals and I had sold the store. The more you crystallize exactly what you want in life, the easier it becomes to make it happen.

When you don't know what you want, you leave it up to someone else to decide what you get.

You might be wondering, "*How do I do this? How do I get clear about what I want and create a more powerful mindset?*"

Sometimes, it takes a defining moment, a moment in time that defines a change in you. A moment you decide.

When I was 30, another company bought the company I worked for. I made a bit of money because I had stock options. We took some of that money, bought three acres of land, and built a dream home.

At one point, our mortgage broker gave me a printout of my mortgage payments, showing me how much interest we had paid to date and how much we would be paying over the entire term of the mortgage.

Around the same time, I read a book called *Rich Dad Poor Dad* by Robert Kiyosaki. When I finished the book, I knew that our entrepreneurial journey was dependant on one thing. I said to my husband, "We need to sell our house."

Within 1 year, we sold our house, bought a house that needed to be fixed up, and cut our mortgage payments in half. With the extra money, we renovated and fixed that house, lived there for 5 years, and sold it for twice the amount we paid for it.

This single decision gave us the freedom to leave our jobs, launch our businesses, buy a house in Florida, and have more financial freedom than ever before.

This happened all because we had clarity on what we wanted most and we were willing to take action to get to our desired state. Do you have clarity? Are you ready for your defining moment and to decide what you really want?

Beliefs

Belief is something you cannot touch or see, but you can feel it and you can think it.

Stephen Covey, in The Seven Habits of Highly Successful People said, *"Begin with the end in mind."*

Once you have clarity around what you want, it is time to tackle the gremlins in your head and build up stronger beliefs. This is the ultimate juice for developing a solid mindset.

Sometimes, in order to change our beliefs, we have to take a good, hard look at them and become consciously aware of our thoughts. When you do this, you can start to see where your thoughts might be holding you back.

You control your thoughts. There is no one in your head thinking them except you. You may be thinking things that you have had ingrained in you from a young age. However, it is never too late to choose how you want to think.

A friend of mine, Sandra Tisiot, has a habit of saying the words *"cancel, cancel"* anytime she catches herself uttering a thought that is not the one she wants in her mind. She says *"cancel, cancel"* in her mind, and then flips her thought to what she wants. This behaviour makes her very aware of her thoughts and very much in control of what she chooses to think.

When you do this often enough, you can change how you think and strengthen your own beliefs deliberately and intentionally.

Think about it. You have already had many situations in your life where you have done things that you did not believe you could do. Make a list of those times and remind yourself of your strength.

Learn to trust yourself more and to have faith in your instincts. Sometimes the thoughts that cross your mind are not real. They are stories your ego tells you to keep you playing small.

Let me show you some examples of where your thoughts might be negatively affecting your mindset and how to flip them to something positive:

Negative Mindset	Positive Mindset
I am afraid I will lose business if I increase my fees.	My customers will pay my increased fees because they know I am worth it.
My family will judge me if I make too much money.	My family will love and respect my accomplishments when I make more money.
My clients will think I am aggressive if I try to sell to them.	My clients will like how confident I am in my sales presentation.
People don't see the value in what I offer.	People can see the value that I offer immediately when they meet me.
People with money are greedy and selfish.	People with money are kind and generous.
I will never reach my financial goals.	I have a detailed plan to help me reach my financial goals.

Do you recognize yourself in any of those statements? When you become aware of the beliefs that are holding you back, you can use the same principal of desired state verses current state, and change them.

Start with small things. Remember the goal of making an extra $100? Start with that because once you make that $100 you begin to strengthen your belief in yourself and have a better chance of changing the way your mindset works.

*If you believe you're never going to get there, then you'll never get there! However, **I believe you can**.*

Overcoming Your Limiting Beliefs

Overcoming your limiting beliefs might feel uncomfortable at first because you are accustomed to thinking self-deprecating thoughts. However, there is one thing I would like for you to consider. How true are your limiting thoughts?

Is it true that all people with money are greedy and selfish? Is it absolutely 100% fact?

No it is not. So why hang on to that belief?

Now the same can be true for 100% of people with money being kind and generous. However, if you get to choose what you believe, wouldn't you rather look at things from a positive perspective rather than a negative one? Especially if you want to build a positive belief in you!

We can choose how we look at every situation. When you start choosing to see the positive in life on a regular basis, deliberately choosing to look for it, something in your life shifts.

The same thing happens when you start to express gratitude daily for all that goes well in your life. Start paying attention to the people you hang out with. Stop hanging around negative people with toxic beliefs and it will be much easier to start cleaning up your own beliefs.

Limiting beliefs are the result of being afraid, and we'll talk about overcoming fear next.

Overcoming Your Fears

Fear can mean different things to different people. For me it depends on what you're afraid of.

- If you're afraid of what people think of you, you may do more and spend more on being accepted.
- If your fear is not having money, you may hoard money and be more averse to risk than someone who is not afraid of loss.

Fear shows up in different ways for different people. Fear exists for everyone; it still shows up for me on a daily basis! You will never eliminate fear but you can learn how to recognize your fear and act in spite of those feelings.

Every time I launch a new training program, I feel fear. I am fearful that no one will sign up, like the content, and that people will think that I did not give enough value.

Are these fears logical and rational? Not really if I take a good look at how things have gone before. Even if they are, it doesn't matter because I know the only way to overcome the fear is to do it anyway.

There is no cure for fear. The only cure for fear is building up more of a belief in yourself than you have fear, and then consciously turning those negative thoughts into positive ones.

What if hundreds of people buy my training programs and I change people's lives? What if everyone loves the content? What if people are blown away by the value I give them? What if people can't stop talking about me for all of the right reasons?

When I catch myself in fear-based-belief mode, I switch up my thinking and force myself to take action.

One of the best things I ever read about changing fear was in Gabrielle Bernstein's book, *Spirit Junkie*, where she says, "*What would you do if you were not afraid?*"

This is how I handle it. I ask myself, "What would I do if I was not afraid?" Then, I muster up my courage and do exactly that.

You will find in business that you face many first times and numerous fears. It's normal and I have found that part of being an entrepreneur is getting comfortable with being uncomfortable.

Examine the Worst-Case Scenario

When I decided to leave my corporate job and open my business, I was really scared. I made good money and had no idea whether I would make money, lose money, be successful, or fail.

In order to move forward, I had to examine and get comfortable with the worst- case scenario.

This is something people don't talk about. Most people tell you to focus on what you want but they don't tell you how to get real. Being positive and focusing on what you want is important; however, I also think that taking a hard look at the worst-case scenario is equally as important. There is a difference between looking at the worst-case scenario and being negative by the way. One is about finding a solution and eradicating fear, the other is about making excuses.

One of my biggest fears about starting my business was in not being able to continue to enjoy the lifestyle that we had.

To understand my fear, I had to understand what it meant.

I was afraid of losing our home. Worst-case scenario meant I could be forced to go back to living in an apartment and have to start over. I had to think about how I would feel if that happened. Would it change who I am? Would I still be employable? Would I still be able to start over and make money even though the worst of my fears had come true?

I decided that it was worth the risk and that I could handle it if that happened. I had been there before and made it to where I was currently so it was possible to do that again. I was prepared to take the risk because

I spent time thinking through exactly what I would do if the worst-case scenario came true.

Sometimes you have to start small to overcome your fears. For me the best way to gain power over fear is to understand what you will do if what you are afraid of actually happens. By identifying the very thing I was afraid of and taking a good look at it, I was able to dissipate the power it had over me.

You can try this, too.

It's the act of seeing *how you would recover* from the worst-case scenario that allows you to no longer feel restricted by your fear. Get yourself into action mode; figure out what you would do if that happened, then you are no longer powerless because you know what you would do.

Remember when I talked about my defining moment with our mortgage and interest payments?

You can have a defining moment at any time in your life. If fear holds you back, this could be it.

This can be the moment when you realize that you really do have complete control over what you fear.

Your ego wants to keep you playing small and is run by fear. Your true self is run by your soul, and your bigger purpose in life is run by faith.

There are two very important things you must know about fear:

1. Fear never goes away. It doesn't matter how successful you are, you will still experience some form of fear.
2. Everything you want is on the other side of that fear.

Embracing Your Fears

Once you've embraced your fear, it gives you power. Fear prevents you from taking action because you're afraid; however, *when you take the power away from the fear, you're no longer afraid so you're more inclined to take action.*

We all know 90% of the things we're afraid of will never happen.

We know that logically, but the fear still prevents us from doing 90% of the things we want in life. How is that rational?

It's not, and the reason that this is so important is that running a business can be scary. You will find that you face fear on a daily basis especially if you are running a business for the first time. There are so many unknown things that you will run into and each one can feel intimidating.

Sometimes you may look at other business people who are different from you and think they don't have fear. I promise you that everyone has fear, and that everyone deals with his or her fears differently.

The only difference is that person has done more work on or taken more action in spite of their fears.

If you don't believe me, ask them how they overcame their fears and listen carefully to what they tell you. You can learn a lot from how others handle their fears. One thing is for certain: they won't tell you they didn't have any.

Focusing on Self-Discipline

Gaining clarity, changing your beliefs, and overcoming your fear are key. To bring it all together, however, you must have self-discipline.

Self-discipline is about taking action. In order to take action repeatedly, you must have self-discipline. You can have absolute clarity, the best beliefs in the world, and be fearless; however, if you don't have the self-discipline to act on what you aspire for your life and business, nothing changes.

Self-discipline is that nagging voice that makes you go to the gym when you don't feel like working out. It's what makes you make the sales call or write a blog post when you don't feel like it. It's getting up in the morning without pressing the snooze button. It's saying "no" to watching TV so that you can focus on your goals.

It's what separates the achievers from the dreamers.

It takes self-discipline and consistent action to build your business and to create an amazing life of wealth and abundance.

If you want to build a business and make money, become self-disciplined in your behaviour and in how you treat money. Learn to treat your money with respect and pay attention to it. One way you can do this is to keep your wallet clean and organized, with all bills facing the same way. The simple act of placing your money in your wallet in a tidy and organized fashion, which demonstrates that you respect money and treat it with care.

As a business owner, another way you can be self-disciplined and respect money is to carefully manage cash flow in your business, measure what matters and not overspend and put your business at risk or in a stressful situation without a careful thought as to how you will repay the money.

In Tony Robbin's book, *MONEY Master the Game: 7 Steps to Financial Freedom*, he talks about your risk threshold. Be aware of the risks that you take with money and the impact that these can have on your life in the exact same way you are aware of the risks of doing other things in life. For example, you wouldn't get in your car and drive after having too much to drink because that would be irresponsible. However, what about money? Are there ways in which you treat money that are also reckless?

If you really want to be a millionaire but choose to spend more than you save, *you will never get there because your actions aren't in alignment with your dream.*

If your dream around money is to be wealthy, you have to ask yourself this one question when you're spending money:

"Is what I'm doing right now going to help me to get closer to my goal or is it going to take me further away?"

Clarity, belief, overcoming fear, and self-discipline go a long way towards developing a solid mindset in your business and around money.

When you do the internal work on your money mindset, you are better able to do the outside, skill-based work of learning how to sell your products or services and how to run your business. Learning those skills will help you accumulate more wealth in your business.

Continue to work on your mindset and how you feel about money. Practice thinking about and feeling all of the good that can happen in your life when your mindset and your money mindset are aligned.

Change your thoughts and your behaviors and you will change your life.

CHAPTER THREE

DEFINING YOUR BUSINESS MODEL

"You must do the thing that you think you cannot do."
— **Eleanor Roosevelt**

T he first action you will take in any business is figuring out what your business model will be. You may do a pilot and test with a proof-of-concept, or you may go all in. The important thing is having a clearly defined business model to guide your actions if you are going to create a profitable and successful business.

So, what is a business model?

Your business model simply is the way you make money in your business. If you want to make six or seven figures in your business, knowing exactly how you will do that is your business model.

Your business model will encompass what it is you sell, the profit margins you make, the distribution channels you choose, and more.

When you are clear on your business model, then all of the action you take aligns with the model you have created and it makes it easier for you to establish financial success and evaluate your model.

In this chapter, I will share with you the model I use in my business, including my own revenue buckets; distribution channels; and my rock, pebble, sand analogy for business growth.

The first time I hesitantly shared my business success publicly, to try and establish credibility by sharing what I had done, someone called me a bragger.

They called me a bragger because I shared the financial results I have achieved in my business. I was a bit taken back by this response. Instead of celebrating my success, or being inspired by it, they chose to attack me.

Society has caused many of us to hold on to beliefs regarding money that need to be shed. As we discussed in the previous chapter, money is NOT the root of all evil, contrary to what you may have been taught as a child and even as an adult.

Money is necessary for you to live and provide for yourself, your family, and your community. If you are starting a business, you need to make money to succeed.

You should never feel you need to apologize for growing a solid, reputable, authentic business that makes money. It is your right and, when you do this, you are sharing the benefits of that business with many other people.

I think it is your responsibility as a business owner to do what you can to grow your business so that you can give back to your community and support the economy. Things like employment, philanthropy, investing, and purchasing, etc. all require money. You cannot employ people without money, you cannot donate to community causes without money and you cannot do business with other businesses without money.

When I opened my consulting business, it was on a bit of a whim.

At a networking luncheon, I casually mentioned that I was going to hold a workshop to teach some of what I know about business. It was a test or pilot to see if I could garner any interest. Fifty percent of the people in the room signed up on the spot!

This was a defining moment for me. I knew I had to get serious because I had just been given a tremendous opportunity to serve and build a business doing something I love.

When you first start, you may have no concept of the financial aspects of running a business or know your beliefs around money. Many women use the excuse that they are not good at math to avoid looking at their numbers in business. In my opinion, that is fear of your results disguised as an excuse.

It's important to understand where your money comes from when creating or growing a business. And, as we discussed in the previous chapter, you'll want to be okay with receiving money and be able to identify your limiting beliefs around money.

Defining Your Business Model

Your business model is about defining the process around how your business will operate and make money. You do this to have clearly defined processes around how you will operate and monetize the business.

Defining your business model and the processes that make your business successful allows you to act from a place of self-discipline instead of fear. When you lack clear processes, it's easy to respond from fear because you don't have a process to back up your response.

Let me explain.

Not long ago, I met with a customer who wanted to buy one of my 90-day Coaching Programs. The customer asked whether the payments for the program could be spread out over the course of a year. Normally, I don't allow payment plans to stretch over such a long period of time.

The fearful part inside of me wanted to say, "Yes," because I didn't want to lose that piece of business. However, the self-disciplined part of me knew that if she couldn't pay within the payment plan time frame, that she wasn't the right customer for me. On that occasion, I chose to stick to the business process that was created to minimize stress around collecting money after the fact.

Once you're clear how your actual business model works and what your processes are, it becomes easy for you to operate from a position of strength rather than a place of fear or loss. It allows you to be more disciplined and decisive in how you show up and how you respond to your customers' inquiries.

Businesses are supposed to make money and they are supposed to make a profit. When you have a lacking money mindset you'll feel bad about making money. Often, a part of you doesn't feel deserving of making money. When this happens to you, you may begin to overcompensate by adding more and more to the product or service you are selling to try and make yourself feel better about receiving money.

I've done this and I have learned my lesson.

Overcompensating in Business

At times I have found myself in situations where I felt the need to over-deliver on my services, over-compensate, or even add more value because of the money I am charging for something. However, sometimes more doesn't equal more, less equals more. I'll give you an example.

While I was working on an outline for a new program called The Social Media Pilot (a training program for business owners), I outlined 10 training modules covering Facebook, Twitter, LinkedIn, Pinterest, and Instagram—all of the social networking sites I thought my customers needed to know about to succeed on social media.

When I asked for feedback from some of the alumni co-pilots who had taken part in my other Pilot Programs, the answer I received was,

'*It's way too much, and I am overwhelmed just reading the outline!*' They took one look and were overwhelmed instantly by the amount they had to learn. The feedback was that it would be better to launch a 10-week program focusing solely on one social network. Less is definitely more in this situation because more would have caused people to get stuck, lose interest, and not complete the program.

When you aren't 100% comfortable with making money, you feel you have to give more to overcompensate for what you are charging. Yet, when you go shopping and spend $100 on a pair of shoes in a retail store, the manager doesn't say, "*Thank you very much, you just spent $100 in our store. Let's give you five pairs for free.*" They accept your money, try to sell you an accessory or handbag, thank you for your business, and you leave.

If your business model (what you offer, and how you make money) is clear from the outset, it will become easier for you to operate the business and eliminate the need to overcompensate.

If you walked into a store and bought a $100 pair of shoes, you would expect to pay for the matching handbag wouldn't you? Your customers expect to pay for extras, too.

Why We Overcompensate

Business owners overcompensate for a number of reasons. Typically, they do this because of the fear of rejection or comparison with other businesses and because the business model and processes are not clearly defined. When this happens, you may find yourself adding more value adds into your products or services because you want to make sure what you are offering to your clients is of a high value to them— or to make sure they'll be really happy with the service. That doesn't mean that it's always the right thing to do.

When you add more and more you sometimes do more harm to your clients than good.

Usually, it's something inside of you that makes you feel like you need to give more than you are being paid for. That's where having the right money mindset to receive the money for the services you offer is important. Understanding your value and knowing your worth will help you get more comfortable with running and operating a profitable business, which we'll explore in the upcoming chapters.

When I first started my business, I really needed to feel good about asking for what I felt my time and knowledge were worth. When I finally came up with a fee structure, someone I know told me I should be charging one-half of that rate in "this" city if I wanted to get any business.

I knew in my gut that I was worth the fee I had set, so....I stuck with it. A few hours later, I sold my first full day of services to a client who asked if she could break it down into eight 1-hour sessions. I said, "Yes," because I was extremely happy to have her business.

However, there was one thing I didn't factor in. When you add in traveling time for eight 1-hour sessions instead of one 8-hour session, every 1-hour session became a 3-hour session. The person who advised me to charge one-half of my rate was being nicer to me than I was to myself because I ended up spending triple the amount of time I had originally planned working with this person due to all of the time it took to travel back and forth.

In business, you have to learn how to say "No" politely and to stick to the way you have things structured. When you compromise the way your products and or services are priced, you end up resenting your client for something you could have said no to. I didn't resent this client, but I did learn my lesson quickly.

As author Brené Brown says, *"Choose discomfort over resentment."*

Make decisions that are aligned with your business model and that support your process and pricing structure, don't make decisions around your desire to please people.

Let me explain. If we go back to the person who wanted to take a year to pay for the 90-day Coaching Program, it was easy for me to say, *"Our process is to only offer a payment plan that does not exceed the length of the program."* It was never about *her* not being able to afford it. It was about the process.

When it's about your business process, you remove your feelings of guilt from the equation. When you eliminate your emotions from having a say in the decision, you will stop over compensating.

Profitability

Part of your business model should include projecting profitability. In other words, know what your profit margins will be. Doing this gives you more clarity around the money you make and keep in your business. Once you know this, you can then ask is adding in an extra product or service going to degrade profit margins or improve them? When you start adding and adding, generally all you're doing is removing profits from your business without realizing it.

Think of it this way. If you know you want your profit margins to be at 30%, you can discern whether adding in that extra product or service is going to maintain your 30% profit margin or reduce it.

My recommendation is that you aim for your net profit to be in the 30% - 40% range all the time and use that factor to make decisions.

If you are a solopreneur, meaning you work from home and don't have any employees or overhead, your profit margins should be significantly higher. If they are not, chances are you have a spending problem and you are resisting admitting it by saying you are reinvesting in your business.

Your profit margin will also be influenced by whether you have a product with a hard cost or a service with a soft or time cost. Your profit margins will be higher if you are charging for time or information than if you are selling physical products at a fixed cost per item.

Be Crystal Clear on Your Business Model

Let's go back to the example of the shoe store. When you buy a new pair of shoes, they don't give you the socks, shoe cleaner, and a new purse to go with them because they feel bad that you bought the shoes. So why would you offer more to "make up" for selling something?

It may be time for you to go back to the basics. In defining your business model, know exactly what elements you will offer in your business and how you will profit from them. This helps you stay on track and tells your customers exactly what to expect.

In defining your model, you will also need to create a budget for sales and expenses. Big corporations have budgets for payroll, training and development, and for expenses. As a small business owner, you may rationalize your spending habits. For example, if your sales are $100K, how much is your payroll budget? How much is your supply and expense budget? How much is your professional development budget?

When you have a budget, you don't arbitrarily spend money because you feel like it. You refer to the budget and make decisions based on the amount of money you have allocated inside of the business for those items. This is another activity that requires self-discipline.

It would be easy for me to hire more people but the budget only allows for us to spend a fixed amount of money on payroll. Let's say my payroll budget is $100K, I could choose to hire three people at $35K per year or four people at $25K per year. In my case, I choose to hire less people at a higher rate of pay because I think their competence level allows us to get more done than the average person because they have a higher skill set. When you pay for a higher skill level, it may cost more but usually the time it takes to do the job goes down because the person is not learning while working on the job.

Business Model: Distribution Channels

It doesn't matter whether you operate a brick-and-mortar retail store or a consulting business, you will have different products and/or services that you sell.

Take a page from the corporate world and think in terms of distribution channels for your business as a starting point. I like to go back to my wireless roots because there we had five key distribution channels that are easy to understand and apply to any business.

They looked like this:

1. Corporate-Owned Retail
2. Independently Owned Retail
3. Third-Party Retail
4. Business-to-Business
5. Direct Fulfillment

Corporate-Owned Retail was designed to meet the needs of the consumer who likes to shop the corporate-owned brand.

Independently Owned Retail was designed to leverage entrepreneurial business owners and the whole community of people who like to support local small business.

Third-Party Retail was designed for people who like to shop the category. They could go to a place like Best Buy and see what all of the different carriers were selling and select that way.

Business-to-Business was designed for businesses that want someone to come to them because they have complex needs that require a dedicated sales rep to serve them.

Direct Fulfillment was designed for people who like online shopping.

Notice how each of these distribution channels was designed to meet the needs of different customers?

Distribution Channels and Service Buckets

What distribution channels do you have in your business? You could have five distribution channels like a wireless corporation or less if you are a small business owner. For example, one could be a speaking channel, one might be online via webinars, and another might be an online store. What are the channels that you use in order to generate sales and how do you define them inside of your business?

When I started my consulting business, I started with a focus on three distinct buckets that I could offer within the different distribution channels.

1. One-on-One
2. One-to-Many
3. Zero-to-Many

The **One-on-One** bucket is designed for me to work with a specific client type one-on-one. This client is usually a woman who makes over $100K a year and has enough disposable income to hire someone like me to help her with strategy and perhaps even implementation in her business. The client sees the value in working privately with a consultant and is not afraid to invest in him or herself— in fact, they do this regularly.

This client does not shy away when she hears what my fee is. The client sees that she is investing in herself by working with me. The same way some people shop at Walmart, others prefer a high-end boutique! This channel in my business caters to the high-end consumer who wants a high level of access. This is typically a coaching client who works with me long term to get help with their business and is committed to generating a return on their investment.

The **One-to-Many** bucket allows me to work with groups of people at a lower price point per person. This bucket typically increases your hourly rate of pay because you create leverage by working with more than one person at a time. If, as an example, you charge $200 an hour to work with someone one-on-one, you should be able to make more than that when you work with a group. My group programs are typically designed so that I can earn two to three times more an hour by working with a group than what I do working one-on-one. The people in the group pay about 20% - 30% of what they would pay me if they worked with me one-on-one.

Here's an example: You can work with one person and make $200 in an hour or you can work with 10 people in a group and charge them each $60. Now you are making $600 per hour for the same amount of time.

The **Zero-to-Many** bucket allows me to do the work once and then let it continue to work for me by generating income when I am not there. I can create an online information product and, once it is complete, it can just sell itself without me doing any additional work. The Pilot Project is a good example of this.

The work in The Pilot Project is complete and aside from a couple of minor tweaks each year, it is good to go every time someone buys the product. The first time we offered this program, 137 people bought it. In essence, I got paid by 137 people to build the program. The second time we offered the program, another 130 people bought it and this time I did not need to do any work. This is a beautiful example of the Zero-to-Many model.

How can this model work for you?

These three buckets typically are priced according to low, mid, and high price points.

What about your business? What channels apply? What are your buckets? What items do you sell in those buckets? How do you price those items and what channels can you sell them in?

Rocks, Pebbles, and Sand

My favorite metaphor for your business is the big rocks, pebbles, and sand science experiment that Dr. Stephen R. Covey shares in First Things First. You've probably seen a similar video to the story where the teacher puts sand in a jar followed by pebbles, then by big rocks. What happens is that he will run out of space in the jar and the big rocks will not fit.

However, if he starts with the big rocks, then adds the pebbles, followed by the sand, he can fit everything into the jar.

It's the same in business. Your big rocks represent your highest revenue-generating items, the pebbles represent your next highest, and the sand your lowest price point, often referred to as low-hanging fruit.

Focus on the big rocks first. This is how you create leverage and grow your business the fastest.

You may be focusing on the smallest rocks and if you are, that is why it is taking so long to build your business. Sand and little rocks add up a lot slower than the big rocks. Many people do this because of their discomfort around asking for the money in a larger transaction.

Identify the items you have for sale in your buckets and figure out what defines your big rocks, pebbles, and sand, then plan accordingly.

It takes the same amount of energy to sell a big rock, as it does to sell sand.

Explore How to Make Money

Identify the ways your business makes money and identify the buckets you make money in. Once you know this, you can determine how much money you need to make in each of those buckets and see what you have to do to grow that piece of the business.

When I ask my clients what they do to make money, often they haven't defined their buckets yet. Therefore, they say "yes" to everything, even if it's not really a part of what they do.

Some people say "yes" to everything they are asked to do because they don't have clarity on their business model. All they are saying "yes" to is money. They don't have a clear strategy or model that differentiates them in the marketplace. This will eventually backfire and create problems. You cannot be all things to all customers.

When defining how your business makes money, start by thinking about the ways you would like to work with people.

First, you have to ask yourself whether you have revenue-generating opportunities that are full-assisted or non-assisted sales (also known as passive income).

Full-Assist

A full-assist sale tends to be a complex sale and can't be completed without you talking to someone. It is a product or service you can't buy without being assisted by someone else. For example, it could be a wireless store where you can't just buy an iPhone, as you need help from a sales associate to renew a contract or change your SIM card. In my business, one-on-one coaching is a full-assist sale. You wouldn't buy my high-end coaching program without first having a conversation with me.

Non-Assist

A non-assist is usually a simple sale. For example, if you're buying an e-book online, you point, click, and download. It's that easy. Or, if you join The Pilot Project, you can just sign up online and our automation system delivers the material to you. A grocery store is another example of a non-assisted experience for the most part. You arrive, walk around, gather the items you want and then pay for them. You don't need someone to assist you with the entire shopping experience.

Who Does the Selling in Your Business?

You will want to ask yourself if what you offer serves people one-on-one, one-to- many, or zero-to-many? Is it a full-assist or a non-assist experience? Can someone else sell your product or service or is it just you?

Depending on your type of business, you may have different opportunities to sell your products and services:

- A sales rep who works for you
- A joint venture partner who benefits from selling products or services with you
- An affiliate member who gets commission from selling your products or services
- You alone

I do some consulting work with big corporations, and there is no one on my team who has the experience to sell those services. This involves me taking the time to understand the needs of the company and putting together a proposal that reflects those needs.

Ask yourself this:

Do you have someone who can sell for you, or is it only you who can close the sale?

I've found that 80% of the sales in my business are generated by me as the business owner, with a small percentage coming through referrals, joint ventures, and affiliate partnerships. Discovering what works for you is a case of trial and error but be aware of one thing...

No One Cares About Your Business Like You Do

Your partners will always prioritize their business first, so don't rely on too many people to make your cash register ring or you will be waiting a long time to reach your business goals.

If you think you can sit back, relax, and not do anything in your business, you will be very disappointed. If it was that easy, everyone would be starting his or her own business.

You are responsible for *generating* sales in your business. If you are expecting someone else to sell for you because you're not comfortable with the sales process, your business probably won't reach the 5-year mark and it definitely won't make the type of money you want to make.

Selling is a skill that you can learn and this skill is necessary for you to be able to build your business. Later in this book, we will cover the basics of learning how to sell so that you get comfortable with selling and making profits in your business.

Your business will struggle until you take full responsibility for generating sales so let's make it as easy as possible for you.

Taking Ownership of Sales

Let's go back to those rocks.

Once you get clear on your channels and buckets, you'll want to examine your rocks, pebbles, and sand more closely.

I've been working on a project generating leads to sell $7 e-books. E-Books that cost $7 don't add up very fast. If I had spent the same amount of energy on selling VIP coaching programs, I would have made significantly more money. So why did I do it? Because, once I've worked out the formula to sell those $7 e-books, it won't require any effort.

You might think this is a mixed message, so allow me to explain:

I can afford to take the time to work on the $7 e-book project because I've built up revenues in other areas of my business and the e-books fall into a bucket that I want to strengthen. My big rocks are under control, now I want to focus on more sand!

If your business is in a start-up phase, you should spend your effort on whatever is going to generate money the fastest before you start focusing on the low-hanging fruit, pebbles, or sand.

Chances are that you're selling the "smallest rocks" because it's the easiest to sell. This could be a limiting belief that is holding you back from growing your business.

Most business owners who focus on selling "small rocks" do so because they lack the confidence to sell the "big rocks." Then, they complain because it takes so long for the business to grow. Can you imagine if all I did was focus on selling my $7 e-book? I would need to sell over 75,000 e-books to come close to my annual sales. That's a lot of e-books and a lot of work!

Think about it. I would need to sell 200 e-books per day, which would require me to send between 2,000 - 4,000 people to my sales page every day if my conversion rate was between 5% - 10%. That's 1.5 million new people a year visiting my website. That, to me, is harder than selling "big rocks"!

When you start with your "big rocks," you grow your confidence in your ability to sell the highest-priced service in your business and you will build your business faster. Don't give up if people don't instantly buy from you either.

Wayne Gretzky said, *"You miss 100% of the shots you don't take."*

Remember that quote, even when people say, "no".

No Does Not Mean Failure

No does not mean failure. When someone doesn't buy what you are selling, don't take it personally because it's not about you. When people fail to sell something at their first attempt, they usually assume their prices are too high, but the truth is it could be any number of reasons.

People may not have the money, it may not be the right time, they may not want what you have, and it could be that you need to improve your sales skills, which we will cover later on in this book. Some of the reasons that people don't buy are within your control, and others are not. If someone says no to you, you need to say next and find someone who wants what you have to offer.

As a business owner, you need to understand sales and conversion rates. Your conversion rate is the percentage of people who buy out of all the people who you present to your product or service. Therefore, if you close a sale 10% - 20% of the time, this means that 1 or 2 out of every 10 people buys.

If that's the case, you should expect 8 or 9 out of every 10 people to say no! It's not personal. Keep going and trust that there's someone else out there who wants what you have to offer. Go find the ones who want what you have.

Build Your Confidence

The Confidence Code by Katty Kay and Claire Shipman is all about women and confidence. In this book, the authors talk about the differences between men and women when it comes to confidence and how we behave based on how confident we feel. One part I took away from the book is this:

When women lack confidence in what they are doing, they do one of three things:

1. They withdraw
2. They withhold
3. They become quiet

Men, on the o ther hand, do no such thing. They believe that they are competent at something even when they are not. They are not afraid of rejection, they don't take "no" personally, and it certainly doesn't affect their confidence or willingness to try again.

This is typically how it goes: A woman will think, *"I didn't close that sale, so I must suck at selling."*

In a woman's mind, it's a logical assumption, but it's the wrong one. With her confidence shaken, she will pull back and not attempt to sell again for a while because she has to rebuild her confidence.

A man, on the other hand, will think, "*I didn't get that sale, so where is the next opportunity?*" They will forge ahead without internalizing and criticizing themselves because they just want to get out there and build their business. If anything, the man will blame the customer for not making a smart choice and won't even consider that it could have been something they did.

If you are a woman reading this book, this is one of the most important things I want you to take away. Do not let a "no" shatter your confidence. It is not about YOU.

In your business you are ALWAYS learning. Just because you don't get what you want the first time you try, doesn't mean you should give up.

I remember one time when I hired a copywriter to help me write a sales page for a new program that I was launching. I went to a studio and had professionally shot videos created. I did everything the copywriter told me to do. I invested a lot of time, effort, and money in working with this individual because I believed that his way would work better than mine.

The morning we sent the email out introducing the program, nothing happened. Not one sale. I was in New York on a trip with friends and panic set in. There had to be some mistake! Something had to be wrong.

It turns out there was. The video player they put on the sales page was not optimized for mobile devices, which meant no one could watch it if they weren't at a computer. Also, the copy didn't sound like me at all, so there was a disconnect for the people who may have been interested in the program. I was disappointed, embarrassed, and felt like such a failure.

I had given my power away to someone else. I didn't believe that my way was good enough. Sure enough, a couple days later, I made some changes and we sold some programs. It was a painful lesson and the biggest thing I got out of it was to trust myself because when I did, the business made money.

You are the leader of your company. Even though at times it feels challenging, it is your responsibility to keep trying until you get it right. It's up to you to keep prospecting, filling your pipeline, closing sales, and selling your products and services because nothing happens until somebody buys.

If you avoid doing these things, you won't end up with the kind of business you really want. That's why I say one of the best ways to build your business is to build your confidence. And, the only way to build your confidence is to take action over and over again, even when you make mistakes.

Three Ways to Build Confidence in Your Business

1. **Understand who your customer really is.** If you're trying to sell to the wrong person all the time, your failure rate will be high and your confidence level will plummet. Take time to really get to know your customer.

   Are they male or female? How old are they? Do they have kids? Do they have pets? What are their hobbies? Do they go to the movies? What do they read? What movies do they like? What is their annual income?

   When you really know your customer, you are in a better place to serve them and when you are better able to serve them, it becomes easier to **sell your product or service.**

2. **Know what value your product or service offers your customer.** What you are selling must help your customer in

some way. It needs to add value, and/or solve a problem or fill a need that your customer faces in his/her life and/or business.

If you don't know what those problems or needs are, and how your product or service helps them, you will struggle to articulate how your product or service can help them and it will be much harder to close the sale.

3. **Know where to find your customers.** Know and go where they are if you want to make it easier for them to find you. Build relationships with people you want to do business with that match your customer profile. Learn how to engage in conversations with these people and build trust. People buy from people they know, like, and trust.

Most people go where they are comfortable. If you want to sell more, move out of your comfort zone and go where your customers are.

Some business owners think that all of their business is going to come from being online. Don't make that mistake.

Social media is a great way to build relationships and to find people but it is not the only place to build your business. You also want to connect the dots from online to in-person and vice versa.

I have found the difference between what I can sell online versus what I can sell in-person to be tenfold.

To put it in perspective, I can sell up to a $5,000 program online if I've built a solid relationship and found ways to give value through sharing content. When it comes to selling anything above $5,000, I have found that most people need to have met me in person in order to say "yes" to a $25,000 or $50,000 sale.

You could be leaving 5 to 10 times your sales potential on the table by not focusing on connecting with the right people in person.

Use online communication to make it easier to connect in person. And, when you meet new people in person, use online communication as a way to follow up and keep in touch. That's how you connect the dots.

CHAPTER FOUR

MEASURE WHAT MATTERS

"Poor is the man whose pleasures depend on the permission of another."
– Madonna

I f business is about exchanging a product or a service for money, it's important that you have the right systems in place to measure those outcomes. Otherwise, you won't know how you are really doing.

If you don't know how you are really doing, you make decisions from a place of emotion instead of fact, and that can get your business into financial trouble fast.

Savvy business owners measure results in their business because they know that those measurements are objective and tell them the truth about what is going on.

I've had several conversations with business owners who admit that they send everything to their accountant at the end of each month and later (several months later) they find out how their business is doing.

They have no idea how their business is doing in sales each month nor can they break it down by week or day nor can they tell me if they were up or down over last year or what their cash flow situation is.

In All of These Cases, the Businesses Were Hurting

As a business owner, doing this is REALLY alarming because it means you are operating in the dark. Just like I gave my power away to that copywriter, if you do this, you have given your power away to your accountant and your outcome is likely to be like mine was—bad.

Measuring what matters is the most important thing you can learn to do in your business, if you want your business to thrive and not just survive. Measuring your financial health is critical to your business success and your business longevity.

It's great that you know that you received 500 comments on your last Facebook post or 32 new "likes" on your Facebook page yesterday, but if you didn't generate any real revenue in your business, you have a problem.

You cannot take Facebook likes and comments to the bank and buy a new car or pay your mortgage, can you?

Measuring what matters is about being able to discern which metrics are the most important in your business in order for you to assess your progress.

I discovered the truth of that really fast when I opened my own store and almost went under.

A couple of months after opening, I found myself in a situation where I owed $100,000 for inventory, and I didn't have the money to pay for it. I had ordered too much for the Christmas season and had not sold enough to recoup the cost of what I had left on hand.

I remember lying in bed thinking, *"This is not good pillow talk. My husband is going to kill me."* In less than 90 days, I had successfully gotten myself to the verge of bankruptcy. It was one of the worst nights of my life. I felt horrible and even though I knew my husband wouldn't "really" kill me, I didn't want to be a disappointment to myself so early in the game.

I was shocked when I found out that I owed $100,000. I wasn't measuring what mattered back then, which means the bill was a big surprise to me.

I learned two critical lessons:

First, I had no clue how to manage cash flow. It's one of the things that *really* matter when it comes to measuring what matters. You might upset a customer but you can always get another customer. If you run out of money, the bank runs out of confidence in you and you're suddenly out of business.

Second, I learned the value of asking questions. As I lay in bed that night agonizing over what I was going to do with that $100,000 bill, I realized I would have to eat some humble pie. The next morning I called my supplier to find out what my options were.

I had to explain that I didn't have the money to pay for the inventory and that much of it was sitting on the shelf in my store. I was embarrassed to have to call and ask them to give me some type of an extension to pay.

In making that call, however, one of the things I learned was that I could restock inventory once a year without incurring a restocking fee. That means I was allowed to return unsold inventory once a year at no cost to me. That enabled me to make the necessary payments right away and fill in the gap by returning the inventory that I didn't need.

That phone call saved my business. Sometimes you need to swallow your pride and ask for help.

Don't get me wrong. Measuring engagement on social media and the number of "likes" you have is an important part of your business *if you're turning "likes" into leads and leads into paying customers.*

But… if you don't have any sales and all you're doing is measuring those likes and failing to learn how to turn them into leads, then you're not measuring something that matters because there are no financial results or outcomes attached to what you're measuring for your business.

Only you can decide what the most important things are to measure in your business.

Businesses are evaluated based on their financial numbers so if you want to build something that lives on, pay attention to those numbers early on.

This can feel emotionally exhausting when you don't understand how or when things are not going as well as you want them to. This is why it is critical to systematize what you measure so that things do not get out of control and you end up owing $100,000.

Six measurements matter to me in my business:

1. Sales and Expenses
2. Net Profit
3. Accounts Receivables
4. Cash Flow
5. Size of My Community (Subscriber List)
6. Website Traffic

Of those six items, below are the three that are critical to review weekly:

1. Sales and Expenses
2. Size of My Community (Subscriber List)
3. Cash Flow—Money in the bank so that I know what our situation is at all times

Getting Started—Measuring

When I speak with business owners about their numbers, sometimes they share with me that they feel a sense of shame and ignorance when it comes to their numbers. They feel like they will never "get it."

I know that's not true and that anyone, even you, can learn how to measure and interpret the numbers in your business. I promise that simple math is all that's required and that neither algebra nor calculus are needed to be a successful business owner.

One of the reasons I created The Pilot Project was to help others learn how to measure what matters in their business. I really wanted to help them overcome the fear of the unknown and to gain confidence in how they look at and interpret the numbers in their business.

When I start coaching a new business owner, one of the first things that he or she is asked to do is to get naked financially. We go through the business owner's numbers in detail to establish a baseline so that he or she can measure his or her future progress.

This is not done to humiliate the business owner; rather, this process is performed for empowerment. When you look at your numbers, see where you are, and see your progress, then numbers become fun! My clients often tell me, "I am learning to love my numbers," which not only lets me know that what I'm doing is working, but also makes me extremely happy.

As a business owner, you can learn more about your numbers by taking a course, a program, working with a business coach or, in some cases, working with your accountant.

If you decide to hire a business coach, don't let his or her title fool you. If your objective is to learn about the numbers in your business, be sure the person you're talking to understands money and metrics in business, as well as *how those metrics actually work.*

Choosing a Business Coach

When you're choosing a business coach to help you with this process, here are some questions you can ask:

- What do you know about managing cash flow in business?
- How do you teach people about cash flow?
- What measurements are important to you in our coaching relationship?
- What numbers have you successfully helped other business owners move?

In The Pilot Project, I share spreadsheets that can help you manage your cash flow one year in advance. This enables you to anticipate and project just how much money you should have in the bank on any given day, 365 days of the year—that's how fanatical I am about managing money and cash flow! If you find that you are always running out of money or dipping into your credit line, chances are you have a cash flow problem just like I did when I first opened my store.

Some of the business owners with whom I've worked with, achieve tremendous results just by reframing how they look at the numbers in their business and what they need to do to change them.

We don't just talk about stuff. We measure what matters.

Remember, the degree to which someone else has succeeded is the degree to which he or she can bring you along.

You don't hire a personal trainer who is unhealthy and unfit. Therefore, why would you hire a financial planner who has no money? Don't hire a business coach who hasn't demonstrated financial growth in their business if that is what you want them to help you do.

Sales, Setting Goals, and Measuring Progress

You can measure everything you need to know on a simple Excel spreadsheet. You will also need some type of system that allows you to keep track of your sales and payments so that you can pull regular reports to see your numbers.

I use two different types of online software to process sales in my business. I can pull reports from each of these programs by date range allowing me to see results in my business by day, week, month, and year. It is easy to access the information and I look at it on an almost daily basis.

Another system that keeps me on track is pulling and submitting my reports at the end of each month for my bookkeeper. This keeps me accountable. Reports of sales and accounts receivables allow her to reconcile my banking so that I know what my net profit is.

Because I use these systems to report sales and I measure cash flow fanatically, it is very easy to measure how my business is progressing every year.

If you want to see things at a glance, you can create a one-page spreadsheet and use it like a dashboard to measure what matters to you. There are three pieces of information that I track:

1. Consulting Sales
2. Coaching Sales
3. Online Sales

I track my results that way because I have different goals in my business for each of these buckets.

I always want to know what percentage of my business comes from each bucket.

It's not just about tracking sales. It's also about setting goals for the sales that you'd like to accomplish each week or each month or for the year in your business by product or category.

This dashboard will allow you to track progress around the goals you have set and make it easy to see what you did for the same month, previous year.

If you want to change the results that you see, *you have to become an active participant in the growth of your business.*

The Benefits of Tracking

You might be thinking, "*This is overkill,*" but let me ask you this:

Do you want to make a little bit of money in your business or do you want to grow your business and create equity?

Statistics and numbers don't lie. They tell you the truth. You are in control of your business when you know what's going on. Knowing where you stand might cause discomfort at times when things aren't going well but at least you know and can take action before things implode.

When you operate your business with blinders on, you have a higher likelihood of going bankrupt because you have no idea what is going on. Many business owners run out of money because they don't pay attention to the numbers in their business.

Measuring what matters really does matter!

You wouldn't get in a car and drive it if the fuel gauge and speedometer didn't work because you wouldn't know how fast you were going or how far you could drive. Why on Earth would you run a business without access to information that is critical to your survival?

When you become intimate with the numbers, you really understand how your business is operating, and you can take some of the emotion out of the decisions you have to make.

SECTION 2

CONTENT PRINCIPLES

CHAPTER FIVE

YOUR CONTENT
IS YOUR CREDIBILITY

"Kind words can be short and easy to speak,
but their echoes are truly endless."
– Mother Teresa

I n today's business, your content is your credibility.

Without a visible online presence, your business will struggle to succeed because today's consumer is conditioned to do their due diligence online first. When consumers hear about you for the first time, they check you out. This means they go to your website and social networking sites to see what you are all about.

Thus, the content you create actually forms the first impression that a potential new customer has of you and your business. In this chapter, we'll cover just why that's the case, and I'll give you some suggestions on how to build a content plan for your business and why it's important to show up as a professional and create content consistently.

Today, everyone uses Google to gain more information about businesses and to explore reviews about products, services, and the people they want to do business with.

It doesn't matter what you're buying. If you're a consumer shopping for a stainless steel stove for your kitchen, you'll Google that stove and look at all the different options that are available. You'll use the information you find to make a buying decision.

You might even do the same thing when selecting a doctor, dentist or hairstylist.

The same applies to small businesses too. It doesn't matter if you're an author, coach, consultant, speaker, healer, network marketer, or if you run a brick-and- mortar retail business, your online content leads people to you and helps you build credibility.

Google Can Be Your Friend or Foe

What happens if you don't publish content?

Something like this: I go to your website to check you out. I see that the last time you published content was 2011. What that tells me is that you might not be in business anymore. Likewise, if I Google you and there's no information about you or your business because you don't have a website or any social media presence, you're basically invisible online, and that tells me that you're not really relevant or you would be there.

Sounds harsh doesn't it? Welcome to the world that we live in today. It's made even worse by the fact that everyone carries a smart phone that is loaded with the most popular social media apps. Not only are they Googling you, they are checking you out on Facebook, LinkedIn, and Twitter, too.

Google can be your friend or your foe depending on what you feed it. If you feed it lots of great content, you can expand both your credibility and your reach so that people can find you. If you don't feed Google content, then that tells potential customers you're not mindful of how people will perceive you and your business online. When I say feed Google, I don't mean it literally. You don't have to "send" anything to these sites. Google and other search engines will find your content, as long as you create it.

It used to be that businesses were found through word of mouth. Now they are found by 'world of mouth' as in www—dot—of mouth, because today people automatically search for what they want online.

If someone says to you, *"Lisa Larter is a really smart business coach and you should check her out."* What are you likely to do? You will most likely check me out and form your own opinion without ever making contact with me personally.

In the old days, what would you do?

- You would have to look up Lisa Larter in the Yellow Pages.
- You would have to call a business or speak with someone to learn more about her products or services.
- You might even have to meet with Lisa Larter to understand what her business offers before making a decision around her credibility.

Google—or the content people find—allows others to be informed of what you and your business are all about, before they ever approach you. You content is selling to people before they have made any contact with you.

That means that absence of content on your website or the wrong content can stop these people from contacting you and inquiring about your business.

How to Build a Content Plan

Building a content plan is essential in your business. However, when you first start out, it's not easy. You can't just publish a blog post and expect the masses to flood in and for your blog to be inundated with traffic, comments, and social shares. *It takes time and effort.*

When I first started blogging, it was super frustrating. I would agonize over what to write about, and then I would work diligently on creating this masterpiece and not one person would comment on or share what I wrote. That was extremely discouraging, and there were many times that I wanted to give up and make excuses as to why blogging was not for me.

The problem wasn't really the blog or the content. It was the visibility that the content was receiving. People didn't know I existed. The distribution mechanism that I had in place was not working for me.

What I quickly realized was that creating the content is only part of what you need to do. The world does not stop the moment you hit publish and run to see what you have written. Even famous, best-selling authors and people as gifted at writing, such as Seth Godin, have a strategy around distribution. And, in order for you to distribute, you must first…DO THE WORK.

You have to build a content plan.

When it comes to creating blog content, the best way to start is to create a framework around when and what you are going to create. This is the framework I suggest you start with:

Framework

When will you publish content?

Decide on the day(s) of the week that you will do this and then stick to that decision—no excuses, ever. Amateurs make excuses and professionals just get it done (we'll talk more on that shortly).

What are the topics you will write about?

Make a list of key categories and then the topics that fit into those categories. If you come up with seven (7) categories, and seven (7) topics within each category, you have just about enough content for one post a week for an entire year.

Decide when and how to create content and what format that content will be. Content can be delivered in many formats, including written, audio, video, or pictorial. You get to decide what works best for your business, and you can use a combination of these formats if that works best for you.

Once you have given this some thought, you can then create a plan around the actual creation of the blog content. I am going to give you some guidelines below for written and video options. These are my guidelines—they are not rules. You can create your own guidelines if these do not work for you.

A tip for always having content ideas, is to keep a list of the questions that people ask you. Your content is there to serve others and by answering questions people have, you create familiarity and show them from the beginning what your business is all about. Always create content from the perspective of serving others.

Written Blogs

Writing a blog may seem easy, but if the last time you wrote something was back in school, it may not be as easy as you remember.

Here are some guidelines to help you:

The biggest hook for your reader is the title and first paragraph.

Have a compelling and catchy title that grabs the attention of the reader. Think in terms of the headings that you see on the covers of magazines. You want your title to grab attention and to be eye-catching for the reader.

If you struggle with creating titles, create a swipe file and every time you see a title that grabs your attention, write it down. You can use other people's titles as inspiration and *model* some of what you do from those titles. I am not a proponent of copying; however, I do believe inspiration can come from looking at what others have done.

Next to the title, it is the first paragraph you write that draws a reader in. Too often, our writing starts soft and then, two paragraphs down is where the juicy stuff is. Look at your copy carefully and start with your best stuff. We live in times where people are looking for instant gratification and are easily bored. The key to getting someone to read the rest of your post is to draw them in from the start. Don't be afraid to re-order paragraphs after you have written your content.

Identify the objectives of the blog post.

What is the key message you are trying to convey? How do you do that? Once you know what the key message is and the points you want to cover, you can write the first paragraph and then, the middle section, which is typically the meaty content portion.

Next, you want to determine how to wrap up your content and create a call to action or identify what the next step is for the reader so that you can create engagement.

Too often, we finish a blog post and fail to engage the reader to participate actively in some way. Some of the methods that you can utilize to engage your audience is by asking them a question, inviting them to leave a comment, suggesting that they share the blog post, read another blog post that relates to the one they just read, or maybe even check out a product or program that you offer.

Seed your products and services where it makes sense.

In every one of my blog posts I try to either seed to a free offer some way to build my list or have a link to a product or program that is a revenue generator in my business. This is done in a skilful way, which aligns with how the blog post is written.

If it doesn't make sense, I don't force this but the majority of the time I can reference a book, training program, or one of my services somewhere and cross- link from my article to that item within the blog post. It is good to have links inside of your blog post so that people can learn more from you, and it is also beneficial for SEO (search engine optimization), too.

Seeding is a subtle way to let people know that you have something else for them. One of the ways I seed is by mentioning my eBook on Building Your Business Online.

We reference the eBook and then link to the sales page in some of my blog posts. Even mentioning it here in this book is seeding. Seeding does not mean hanging out a big red sale sign and saying, "Hey, come buy my eBook." It is subtle and written into the article in a way that makes sense for the reader.

Other tips that might help you when it comes to writing blogs are word count, key words, images, and themes.

Word Count

Use as many or as few words as you need to express your point. However, don't go on and on or you will lose the reader.

Write your post and then edit it. People often write and edit at the same time, however, when you do that it takes longer and you never quite get the same flow or outcome as when the editing is done separately. I prefer to keep my blog posts around the 500- to 700-word mark as a guideline but there are exceptions to this as I have had some very good results from long blog posts. I know from contributing to the *Huffington Post* that they request articles between 500 and 1,000 words, and I would assume they know best!

Keywords

Know what your keywords are and use them in your blog content. If, for example, your blog is *Five Ways to Make Facebook Work for Your*

Business, then you should mention the keywords Facebook and business in your blog content.

Each business has different keywords. Make a list of those associated with your business and intentionally use them where you can so that when your customer is searching for those words they can find you through those keywords.

Images

Use images that are graphically appealing and that you own. Don't take images off Google or any website without purchasing a license to use it because everything else is stealing and it is illegal.

When you upload an image to your WordPress site, use a relevant file name and save the image with appropriate keywords in the title and alt text too. People search Google using keywords and often filter by image. When they view your image and click on it, they will be directed to your website. Too often people upload images that only have numbers associated with them and they miss the opportunity for those images to lead people to their website.

Keep It On Brand

If you have a clearly defined brand, your images, copy, and voice should align with that brand. If you are not sure how to do this, hire someone who is good in branding and get them to help you. Your images should all align with the look and feel of your website. Remember, the graphics you use, create a first impression when someone is looking at your website and evaluating your business for the first time. Brand is not just about what things look like, brand is how people "feel" about you and your business.

Themes

Pay attention to what other people are doing for blog posts. Do you remember when I suggested that you have a swipe file?

I really like posts that are themed like this:

- 5 Ways to _____ so that you can _____
- 25 Reasons to _____
- The Number One Reason _____
- 3 Ways You Can Learn How to _____

I also like posts that have a bit of allure in the title, for example:

- "Why Free Is Too Expensive"
- "How Bartering Is Bleeding Your Business"
- "The Two Most Important Words in Blogging"

You want your titles to be clever but not so clever that they don't make sense. You should always be able to identify the message or keyword in every title.

Video Blogs

To a certain degree, you can follow the same format as written blogs when you create video.

1. Have a great title that contains the right keywords so that it can be searched and found on YouTube.
2. Make your intro snappy so people want to watch more. Don't go on and on for five (5) minutes about who you are or your viewer will stop watching.

3. Teach high value content, usually no more than three key points.
4. Keep it under five (5) minutes if you can.
5. Add a call-to-action in the wrap up.

In training development, there's an expression that goes like this:
"Tell them what you are going to tell them."
"Tell them."
"Now, tell them what you told them again."
This works well in video, too. Let me illustrate in a simple format:

1. I am going to show you three ways to get more people to like your Facebook page.
2. The three ways you can get more people to like your Facebook page are:
   • Add a Facebook Like Box to your website so people can like the page from there.
   • Use Facebook Ads to get more likes specifically targeting people in your market.
   • Invite all your friends by using the build audience option at the top of the page.
3. Just to recap, the three ways to get more people to like your page are: you need a Like Box, an ad, and to invite your friends.

Your video does not need to be long and drawn out. One of the best tips I learned from a client of mine to help you to remember what you want to say is to set up a flip chart next to your video camera with the key points you want to cover. It's a bit like cheating but it helps you not be so nervous about forgetting your message when you are recording.

When I do a webinar (live video), I always have slide notes on my computer screen that I can glance at while I am speaking to my video camera. It helps me stay on track and gives me the liberty to also be authentic and real in how I teach my content.

People consume content because they want information. That is why content marketing is also called information marketing. The content, or information you create, is to help your customer solve a problem he or she has and to help you build credibility around what your business does.

Always keep your audience in mind when you are creating this content. The acronym I share with my clients is to be SWIIFT, which stands for "See What's In It For Them."

Most people fall into the WIIFM trap. WIIFM stands for "What's In It For Me." When you create content, it's not about you. It is always about your customer.

You can also be SWIIFT when it comes to how you use social media, too. Pay attention to your customers and the people you would like to be your customer. You stand out by just applying the SWIIFT approach.

Content Plan

When I work with my clients we create a content marketing calendar in an Excel spreadsheet and across the top we map out all the months of the year, holidays, special events, etc., and then down each of the monthly columns we list the dates of publication for each blog post.

In a separate column, we list all the topics and ideas, then we take those ideas and map them out on this calendar for the year.

When you create a visual guide like this to help you with content, all of a sudden it is not so hard to do because you have a plan and you know what to do next. You can get a blank copy of the content marketing calendar we use here: PilotToProfit.com/FreeTools.

Last, if you really dislike creating content, you can hire someone to help you. You can find people on Elance, oDesk, or even a virtual assistant (VA) who loves to write to help you create content.

If you are better at speaking your content—you can record it, have it transcribed, and then edit what you said. One of the traps people get into is they think they have to do everything themselves, but you don't. You can hire VAs from all over the world to do the things you don't like to do. Just ensure it is quality content that you would want a potential new customer to read, because your content is your credibility.

Another approach, if you struggle to come up with ideas, is to ask a client or someone on your team to give you a list of suggestions. I did this when I was looking to create a list of topics that would be interesting for videos.

The individual I asked came back with a list of 20 different ideas that I could easily speak about and many I never would have thought of myself. One example she gave me was to do a video about the right time to quit your job and start your business full time. I never would have thought of that because I am too close to what I do to consider that topic. In essence, other people see your business expertise differently than you do and can be a great source of content ideas.

There are resources all around you that can help you create content. If you can't afford to hire someone, find an intern and mentor that person in exchange for a bit of help.

The one thing I know for certain is this:

It will be much harder for you to grow your business, utilize email and social media marketing to increase traffic and sales if you don't have content to demonstrate your credibility and skill level.

Content Is Credibility and Distribution Is King

Your content runs the risk of sitting unfound, unread, and unshared if you do not have a solid distribution plan.

Your distribution plan is a part of what helps you get your thought leadership out into the world.

Notice that this is another area where you may also encounter some mindset issues. They might sound like. "I don't want to bug people by sharing too much or I am not sure if my content is good enough."

When I first started using email marketing in the form of a weekly newsletter to distribute my content, I was apprehensive. What I really wanted was to generate revenue from the weekly mailing of my email newsletter. I was not so concerned about content and, at the same time, I had my own mindset issues around emailing people.

They went like this…

- What if mailing weekly is too much?
- What if people don't like what I say and think I am bothering them?
- Who do I think I am to have an opinion on this stuff?
- I should have started this a long time ago. It's too late for me now.
- Other people are doing this way better than me.

Yes, this was some of the chatter in my head and maybe this is what you are thinking, too.

Next, after the chatter and excuses, came the *analysis paralysis* about what should go into this weekly newsletter.

My approach back then was simple: sign up for a bunch of other people's newsletters, make a list of what they were doing, and then build the biggest, baddest newsletter out there. This would fill my cup with the confidence of over-delivering and completely overwhelm my readers.

It would also ensure that I always had an excuse for why I couldn't get it done because it was too much for me to do.

Sound familiar?

Your newsletter is the vehicle that allows you to distribute your content to people. It should be easy for you to do this and the more layers and steps you create, the more difficult you make it.

The first step is to build your list. Later in this book and in my programs, I teach you how to do that so that your mailing list is legal and responsive.

The second step is to create content people want to consume. This becomes relatively easy when you have a content plan to guide you on what to do each week.

The third step is to distribute the content. The vehicle for that distribution is email and social media marketing.

Self-Discipline

Self-discipline shows up in many areas of your business, including content creation. Having a content plan is only effective if you do what you say you are going to do and produce the content in accordance with the schedule to which you commit.

You'll want to be professional and have the self-discipline to be reliable around the production and distribution of your content. This means you behave like a professional, not an amateur.

Basically, it's called showing up.

In Steven Pressfield's book *Do the Work,* he talks about the difference between an amateur and a professional being in the amount of action they take.

A professional says they are going to email you weekly and they email you weekly.

A professional says they are going to send five videos, and you receive five videos.

An amateur only sends content out when they feel like it.

Elbert Hubbard said, "*Self-discipline is the ability to make yourself do what you should do, when you should do it, whether you feel like it or not.*"

I am a professional business owner and I am an amateur athlete.

When I say I am going to do something in my business, I am going to show up and do it because I know my business will not succeed without me taking action and keeping my word. When it comes to exercising in my personal life, I'm a bit wishy-washy. I don't show up like a professional in that area of my life, and I usually only exercise when I feel fat or lethargic.

You won't get the results you want in your personal or professional life unless you show up and behave like a professional.

Three Keys to Self-Discipline

Self-discipline is about you. If you want to become more self-disciplined, I suggest you start with these three things:

1. Work on your business.
2. Work on yourself.
3. Don't feed the fears.

Work on Your Business

You have to work *on* your business not just *in* your business.

Have a strategy and a plan with *no more than three clear priorities*. As an example, my three clear priorities are:

1. Increasing the size of my community and establishing strong relationships with those people.
2. Increasing annual sales in the business year over year.
3. Increasing sales specifically in online training programs to help more business owners be profitable.

Whatever I'm doing in the business I ask myself whether it aligns with one of these three priorities. Not everything can be a priority in your business.

Work on Yourself

"Your level of success will seldom exceed your level of personal development, because success is something you attract by the person you become."
—Jim Rohn

I read every single day.

People always say to me, "How do you find time"? I don't find time to read; I *make time.*

I get up early *every day.* I have an hour every morning before I do anything else where I read, journal, and/or sit quietly and meditate. Every day I make sure that I have time to read something that feeds my mind. This practice gives me strength, knowledge, and confidence even in the face of fear.

It also keeps my health in check. Your health is important if you want to build a business. I have had Crohn's Disease most of my life. Stress plays a big role in how active my disease is. By working on me, and taking time to look after my emotional and physical health, I am a stronger business owner and more able to keep my autoimmune disease in check.

Don't Feed the Fears

In Chapter Two, which discusses your mindset and your money mindset, I talk about visualizing the worst-case scenario and working out strategies around that, bearing in mind that *90% of what we are afraid of fails to materialize.*

Fear happens in business for everyone, not just you. It may be the fear of failing, the fear of not being liked, the fear of making a mistake, the fear of not being perfect, the fear of being compared, or the fear of not being good enough.

There are so many ways that we experience fear in our mind; however, you can choose to feed your fear or fuel your positive mindset. Reading is one of the many ways that I fuel my mindset. By reading, I am inspired to take action because I am constantly learning something new. Building your confidence as a business owner and learning to act in spite of your fear is an important part of your path to success.

Signs You Are Feeding Your Fear

You will know when you're feeding your fear because you revert back to the worst-case scenario, playing it over and over again in your mind. For example, when I'm preparing for a talk at a conference I'll start to fear that nobody will show up.

I start playing that loop over and over again.

The only way to escape the loop and the fear is to say, *"Lisa, stop it,"* and start to act.

What will I do to fuel action rather than feed fear?

- Create an invitation to my talk.
- Send those invitations out to people who I think should be there.
- Go online and connect with people who are talking about the conference and invite them, too.

I become pro-active about my talk versus feeding my fear and allowing that fear of no-one showing up to become a self-fulfilling prophecy.
Don't feed your fear, fuel your actions instead.

CHAPTER SIX

EMAILS MAKE YOUR BUSINESS MONEY

"There are people who have money and people who are rich."
– Coco Chanel

Have you ever read an email that made you really mad? Or better yet, one that got you all teary eyed with emotion?

You haven't made it this far in your life without understanding the power of communication skills. What you might not realize, however, is just how much money is tied to your communication skills in business.

In this chapter, I'm going to show you how to hone your communication skills to develop your email marketing success, understand more about subject lines and lead-ins that will encourage your audience to open the emails you send them and, most important, how to build a community rather than a list.

Why Is Effective Communication Important?

People resonate with you when you become an effective communicator. Not everyone will resonate with you all the time, however, but the more skilled and intentional you are with your communication skills, the better chance you have of connecting with the right people.

When you are vulnerable and open in your communication, people become more endeared to you and your business because they feel like they know you and can relate to your words.

Think about the books that you've read. There are some that caused you to smile, laugh, or even cry. Then, there are those that bored you, you got nothing from reading, or couldn't even finish. What was the difference?

It was likely that something was missing in the author's communications skills. They lacked the ability to draw you in and engage you fully. As a content creator, you want to hone your skills and be able to tell a story, engage your readers, and evoke emotion.

The goal of your writing should always be to communicate in a way that causes people to feel your words and really get the meaning behind your message. Words can move others when done thoughtfully and with intent.

How your write something, how you say something, and even your body language sends a distinct message to others. The reason I say there is money tied to your communication skills is because your communication skills attract people to you. Understanding how to write copy or blog content that communicates a message that inspires people can differentiate you in a significant way.

Zig Ziglar, who I had the honour of meeting and who was a profound communicator said, *"Encouragement is the missing ingredient in most people's lives."*

Communication is how you can encourage and inspire people.

Let me give you an example. When I launched The Pilot Project, there was no fancy sales page, just an idea that I thought could help people. One morning, in the shower of all places, I had this idea in my head that wouldn't go away. I kept thinking I needed to teach people about eight specific business concepts. The message was loud but I felt uncertain because I was known for teaching social media— not business building skills.

When I finished my shower, I wrote down my ideas.

I started by posting a simple message on Facebook asking others if my ideas resonated with them. They did.

Then, I wrote a heartfelt email about the challenges of starting your business and I explained how I wanted to help. No fancy sales page, no creative marketing, just an email and an option to buy the idea I had for this program.

After sending that email, 137 people bought the program I had thought up in the shower.

Writing copy in a way that conveys emotion doesn't mean creating sob stories. It means that people resonate and feel what you're saying. Humour, sadness, happiness, and inspiration can all be felt through the way you write and the way you communicate when you speak.

You can evoke people's emotions and connect with them when you are skilled in your communication. People buy from those they know, like, and trust. Your communication will cause people to decide if they want to know, like, and trust you more.

Below are some of the most effective ways of communicating.

Email Marketing

Email is by far the most effective way to distribute content and communicate your business message. I believe this because I measure it against all of my social media postings to see what generates the most revenue in my business.

The vast majority of people check email on their smartphone before they even get out of bed in the morning.

Why do I email? It's simple:

- Email delivers my message directly to your personal Inbox.
- You signed up to receive email from me so you expect and even look forward to it.
- Everyone I send email to sees it as opposed to a social media channel deciding who sees it because you control your inbox.

When you send email, the receiver decides whether they want to open and read your email or press delete. When you post on Facebook, Facebook decides whose newsfeed your content ends up in, so basically you are giving your power to Facebook.

Many people create content and then let it sit on their website, hoping that it gets found. Then, they think they have failed because no one comes to read what they have created. What they don't realize is that everyone is busy with their own life and has their own different and important agenda. The only way you can really get people to see what you've created is to send it directly to them.

What Is Email Marketing?

Email marketing is sending information via email to the people who have subscribed to your mailing list that serves and adds value in some way for them. When you send content that adds value on a regular basis, from time to time you can offer an opportunity for those people to buy something.

Email marketing is a form of marketing that allows you to build a community versus just a list. I believe when you add value on a regular basis and you respond to the messages people send back to you, that you are establishing relationships. To me that is what builds a community over a list, caring about people versus just the number on your list. When someone opts into your mailing list, it is because he/she is interested in the information that you are sending. If he/she opts into your mailing list and it takes you 2 years to send your first email, he/she will have forgotten who you are and why he/she is on your list. This is why, mailing when you say you will, matters.

Email marketing needs to be consistent in order for it to be effective. If you say you will mail weekly, do it. If you say it will be once a month, do it. My preference is weekly because there is a good chance that if you wait for 2 weeks to email me that I may have moved on and lost interest. It doesn't matter if you are a realtor, psychologist, author, retailer, or online marketer—you can build a community and add value using email marketing.

As a business owner, when someone wants to hear from you, you want to communicate with him or her as quickly as possible because that is what they are expecting from you.

The person who subscribed to your email list is an adult. If they feel like you are emailing them too often, they will unsubscribe on their own so long as you are abiding by CAN-SPAM, SPAM or CASL laws and provide them with an easy way to do so.

And, don't get emotional over unsubscribes. They are a normal part of the process. Just like with sales, it isn't personal. There could be any number of reasons why this person no longer wants to receive your emails. You only need to be concerned if all you get are unsubscribes. If that is the case, there is definitely something flawed with your communication style or you are mailing too frequently.

Here are some things you need to consider before beginning your email marketing:

- What day of the week will you mail?
- How will you connect in a way that is personal and personable?

- What information will you share?
- What email marketing tool (program) will you use?
- Who will do the work to make sure this happens?

Email marketing really comes down to having the self-discipline we discussed in Chapter Five. When I first started, it was hard to do and that is why I hired someone to help me accomplish this task every week.

When it comes to how often you email and what you include, it really depends upon your audience. However, my experience with email marketing has been: less is more. I used to send two regular mailings each week:

Shop Talk—including a simple intro plus a video blog.

Newsletter—this included a longer intro, a featured article (blog), a product offer, and a bio box.

Through trial and error I have found that my audience wanted simple, not overwhelming. Now, I send only one email a week and it's pretty stripped down. The most effective emails are usually when they are simple and focus on one thing because that makes it much easier for the reader to consume. People are busy and like to read information in small, bite-size chunks. When you give them too much to read, they feel overwhelmed and they will defer the reading to later, which usually doesn't happen.

Make Your Email Marketing Communication Simple

Write an introduction that is personable and leads into the piece of content you are sharing. You can share the entire piece of content or you can set up a Read More button that takes your reader over to your website.

Remember when I said you have to measure what matters? The results of your email marketing are one of the most important things you can measure because they are linked directly to your sales.

If your goal is to send traffic to your website, then always use a Read More link or have a link in your copy for readers to click on. These links will allow you to see how many people clicked over to your website so that you can measure the effectiveness of your copy and the effectiveness of where you placed the link.

In addition to how many people clicked the link, you will also be able to measure your email open rates, which are dependent upon your subject lines. Therefore, the better the subject line, the higher the open rate. This again is where simplicity makes a difference. Most people view email on their mobile device and because of that, they only see a limited number of characters for a subject line. It should be short, catchy, and encourage them to open the email.

Mobile Subject Lines and Lead-Ins

One of the challenges you may experience with your email open rate is that you may have forgotten about the mobile screen. The screen on a mobile device is smaller than your computer, which means that you view fewer characters at a glance.

For example, when you look at an email on an iPhone you see a subject line and the first two lines of what is written in the email.

There are approximately 32 characters (including spaces) that show up in your subject line and 32 characters x 2 rows in your first two sentences.

That means that your 32-character subject line and the first 64 characters of the sentence you lead with in your email have the power to make someone open or delete your email.

For example, Hub Spot sent this email:

'Free Guide: An Introduction to Twitter for Business.'

Short and simple, but all I see on my iPhone is:

'Free Guide: An Introduction to Twitter…'

I see 38 characters (including spaces) because the font size on my phone is small.

Most people have their font set to the largest size, and they see:

'Free Guide: An Introduction to T…'

That's 32 characters. That means that the first 32 characters (including spaces) are the MOST IMPORTANT words in your subject line. Are you looking for an introduction to T?

Don't waste that space by putting {Newsletter from My Business} in front of your subject line or guess what? No one is going to open up and read your email because there is no curiosity around the topic you are writing about.

Most people use mobile phones so they can view email on the go. That means you have to be sure that you use those characters wisely.

My advice is this:

- Pay attention to subject lines that make you curious.
- Pay attention to why you feel compelled to open some newsletters and not others.
- Don't use subject lines that are misleading. I'll explain why shortly.
- Take time to review the first two lines that show up as the "preview" in the email. This is the second most important part of getting people to open your emails.

In the Hub Spot email, it says:

"Take advantage of Twitter to grow your marketing with this free gui…."

That is exactly 68 characters. The first 68 are key, pay attention to what you say first. In this case, it is the difference between a guide and a "gui"!

I Was In A Funk

This is an example of an email subject line that I sent out. There was an incredibly high open-and-response rate to this subject line "I Was In A Funk," which continued with:

"Dear...Last week I was in a real funk. One of those places where I was..."

Most people who look at "I Was In A Funk" will wonder what I am talking about. They'll want to know more, they'll want to read what was going on, and they'll open the email to find out.

Sometimes you receive emails from people with random copy about how you can unsubscribe in the first two lines or you may get emails where the subject lines are the same every time with the juicy stuff at the end. If that's the case, there's no compelling reason for anyone to open the message because it always looks the same.

The first 100 characters in your communication are key—the 32 in your subject line and the 64 in your first sentences are the most important words you use to get someone to open and continue reading.

That is the prime real estate in any email you send out and often, the most overlooked.

Avoid Trickery

For your email marketing to be successful, you want to evoke curiosity while you're communicating with people *but you do not want to use trickery.*

Curiosity and manipulation are different. Manipulation is a juicy lead in and 64 or more juicy characters with no depth.

What I mean by trickery is this. Maybe your subject line says:

…'I'm so sorry' and your next sentence says:
…'I'm so sorry I need to apologize' and the next part says:
…'I should have told you before, I'm writing a book.'

In that case, you used that lead-in to trick me into seeing what else you had to say because you want to sell something to me.

Trickery does not endear people to you; it makes them feel played.

People don't like to feel played and if you use these tactics, they will not want to hear from you.

Take time to write your most compelling copy to interest people in the real legitimate message you're writing them about.

People are inundated with email. As I sit here, I have 2,240 unread emails in my Inbox. Therefore, if you want my eyeballs on your email, it's got to be important enough for me to give my time and attention to and I'm no different than anyone else.

People don't love being inundated with email. People scan emails to see what they want to read. If you want people to open and read your email, your communication needs to be good enough to make someone want to read more *otherwise, they'll delete it.*

As I mentioned in Chapter Five, Your Content is Your Credibility, when writing online, people often don't *order* their writing to make the best impression. They lead with their first paragraph being soft yet, if you continue to the second or third paragraph, they have something brilliant to say.

Look at what you've written, get a highlighter, and ask yourself what's the most important thing you've just said, then move it up. Otherwise, you risk people scanning through their Inbox, deleting your email, and losing the opportunity to serve and add value through your work and your business.

Essential Tips to Help You Get Started

When sending emails with effective mobile subject lines and lead-ins, my advice is this:

Long emails are a thing of the past. Your email only needs to be as long as necessary to convey your message. Don't write for the sake of feeling like something needs more.

Send people one simple thing rather than whole bunch of things. Avoid including an introduction, a testimonial, a featured article, an upcoming event, and something that you're selling—it's too long.

Human attention spans are shrinking. It's even been said that we now have a shorter attention span than a goldfish! That's why I suggest that you make your email a solo communication piece versus a digest.

If you have five key pieces of information that need to be communicated in a 15-day period, you're better off sending your emails every 3 days for 15 days rather than sending one email with five things in it. Inevitably, the reader will miss something when you give them too many things to focus on.

Dailies, short and simple emails sent out each day, can be successful. Some strategists and marketing gurus think that dailies are awful but Seth Godin, Notes from the Univers, and The Daily Love have proven them wrong. They send a short email every single day that I am sure millions, of people read.

Another thing to keep in mind is don't pitch all the time. People love to buy but they hate to be sold to and sending emails only focused on selling instead of serving is just not cool.

When you compose your email, write to one person and imagine talking to them as you write your copy. When you shift your thinking from writing to "the list" to writing to an individual in your community, there is a different energy around how you communicate. It becomes more intimate and your reader will feel like they matter to you.

Own Your Community

You don't necessarily own your community on Facebook or Twitter. In order to get your audience to move from social media to your list, you need a tool to get them to actually want to subscribe to hear from you on a regular basis.

One of the most effective ways I have found to accomplish this is to offer something of value for free on social media and then pay to advertise to the people you would like to have subscribe to your community.

When you own your community, it means that you have permission to communicate with them via email on a regular basis. You own the right to communicate with that database provided you have express consent.

Let me put it into perspective. When I share a piece of content on my Facebook page, it's usually viewed by less than 5% of the people who like my page. When I share a piece of content via email, my open rate is around 20%. There's a big difference in the visibility you are getting when you send via email versus posting your content on Facebook.

Let's do the math and see what this looks like.

If you have 1,000 people subscribed to your list and 20% open your email, then 200 people read what you sent. If you are selling something and you have a 10% conversation rate, 10% of the 200 or 20 of those people will buy.

If you have the same number of people who like your Facebook page and only 5% see your content, that translates to only 50 people. If 10% of those 50 people buy, that's only 5 sales.

Do you see the difference?

For the record, if you are getting 5% visibility on your Facebook page without paying for ads, **good job**. The average I am hearing as I write this is less than 1%.

Below are two golden rules:

1. **Communicate Value in Some Way**

   When you offer something that's of value and you're authentic, people want to hear from you! You want to write so well and add so much value that people miss you if you stop emailing them.

2. **Build a Relationship**

   In order to build a relationship with your community, you must use good copy. If you don't consider that there is a human being with feelings on the other end reading what you've sent, you will struggle to build a relationship with these people.

   Remember, you are writing to one person, not to a group because it's one person reading your communication. They need to feel like you are speaking directly to them. Your email arrives in their Inbox. They read it alone. They do not read it with "you guys." Write as though you are talking directly to that one person.

Build a Community, Not a List

Have you ever gone to a networking event, exchanged business cards with someone, and suddenly found yourself on their mailing list? That person is building a list, not a community.

To successfully build your business online, you need an email list that enables you to directly contact the people who have expressed an interest in your product or service. There is a right and a wrong way to build this list.

Most marketers will tell you, "Build the list, build the list!" Some people will take anyone with a pulse on their list. However, that's not what you want to do.

That is the wrong strategy and here's why.

A small list with people who want to hear from you is more valuable and responsive than a colossal list with a ton of people who don't care about what you are doing.

When you are creating content, try to think of the subscribers on your emailing list as your community or your tribe. In my case, I am 100% confident that I can email my community, ask a question, and receive tons of replies. Likewise, I can post in my Facebook group, ask for feedback on an idea that I have for an upcoming program, and I'll receive feedback. I will get lots of it, even though my community is not large.

These are real people in your community, not just a bunch of faceless names. You can build a relationship and have credibility with that community by consistently offering value and great content for them.

There's reciprocity; there's back and forth. I help them and they help me.

The more connected you are to your community, the more financial value you have in your business.

Here I am writing this book and I already have people saying they can't wait to read it although they don't know what it's about. That's the value of community. Perhaps you're one of those people reading it right now, if so— thank you for your support in all that I do. I value and appreciate you.

In *Good to Great*, author Jim Collins writes about getting the right people on the bus because if you have the right people on the bus they don't care where the bus is going; they just want to be on the bus.

The same applies when you're building your subscriber list. If you have the right people within your community, they trust you and will put their hands up for whatever you do because they believe in you.

Your community is filled with people who are your advocates; your list is just email addresses.

Building a community is about three essential areas—*nurturing, respect, and access.*

If someone emails me, I'll respond with a reply. If someone posts a comment on my blog, I'll acknowledge it. If someone posts a question on Facebook, I'll respond with an answer. Replying to comments and inquiries in a time-sensitive manner is something that I'm very passionate about.

However, not everyone does this. I've emailed people whose list I am on and they have never responded to me. In some cases, I've even received an auto responder telling me that the Inbox they email me from is NOT monitored. This is not a great way to make someone feel like you care.

Let me break down the three areas for you.

Nurturing

To me, nurturing means:

1. Show up when you say you're going to whether it's in Inboxes, in a Facebook group, in a Google Hangout, etc.
2. Demonstrate credibility through the content you create.
3. Do what you say you're going to do, and do it when you say you're going to do it.
4. Respond, validate and acknowledge others whenever you can.

That's nurturing the relationship with your community.

If I say that I'm going to send you an email every Thursday morning, I'll send you an email.

If I get a reply to one of those emails, you'll receive a response from me. That demonstrates another level of nurturing.

By responding, I am telling you that I care that you sent me a message or gave me feedback. The same applies when someone leaves a comment on my blog or through social media; they are acknowledged. This makes people feel good about the access they have to you. They feel you actually care about them.

You may reach the point in your business when you are so busy that you don't have the time to respond to every single person, and I get that. However, you can still put systems in place to help respond.

Look at it this way. If you walked into my retail store, I would say, "Hello." I would acknowledge your visit to my store. Therefore, if you walk into my online business through my Inbox, I will value you in the same way and do my best to make you feel welcome and address your needs.

Not everyone shows up at the same time. However, when they decide to show up and make a concerted effort to interact with you, acknowledge them in some way.

Respect

People want to feel like they are valued and appreciated, period. It is a basic human need.

If someone makes an effort to communicate with you, the best way to demonstrate respect is to respond. There are definitely some exceptions when people you don't know are emailing you cold to pitch or spam you, but for the most part, legitimate and sincere people deserve a response.

If I send you an email and you reply to me, I don't want you to feel like you're on a list, I want you to feel like you're part of my community.

I want you to feel *respected*. When you respond to my email, I feel obligated to personally respond to you because you are part of the community that I'm trying to build and responding and respecting you are part of my values.

If your business is too big and busy to do that, you should have a process in place so that someone on your team is able to respond on behalf of your company.

Treating people with respect is essential to building your community.

Access

Someone recently visited my Facebook page and sent me a private message to my Facebook page Inbox. She shared with me her vulnerabilities about creating videos and asked me if I felt the same when I first started out. She also asked for an example of how I handled this discomfort because she considers me a role model in terms of how I run my business.

I'm busy and she's not my client. She's not paying me to answer that message but I did because she is part of my community, I respect her and it took 2 seconds to do.

I acknowledged her for her feedback, I validated her feelings of vulnerability because I experienced them when I started creating videos, and I sent her a link to a website I built to help people create videos with confidence.

That's an example of access and, while it only took a couple of minutes of my time, it made a difference to that person in my community. You can make a difference to people in your own community when you acknowledge and respond to them.

If you don't want to respond to people on your Facebook page or offer them that type of access, the solution is simple—disable your Facebook page Inbox and don't make it available.

How you treat people matters, and responding to them on the channels you distribute your content on is your job if you really want to build your community. There is no point in trying to create content, sending out emails, having social media profiles for your business, and building up the size of your subscriber list if you have no intention of engaging and building relationships with your potential customers.

If you can't build relationships, you will be one of those people who says, "Social Media doesn't work." It's not social media, it's how you are treating those people and in the next chapter, I am going to go deeper with explaining how to make social media work better for your business.

Would you like to learn more about building a highly engaged community using Facebook groups? Go to www.PilotToProfit.com/FreeTools and I will share a simple step-by-step checklist on exactly how I have built my own group and give you the community guidelines that keep my group from being filled with spam.

SECTION 3
SOCIAL
PRINCIPLES

CHAPTER SEVEN

SELLING ON SOCIAL MEDIA

*The richest people in the world build networks;
everyone else is trained to look for work."*
– Robert Kiyosaki

S ocial media is the new magic pill that will solve all your business
needs. And, if you believe that, well...We have a problem.

You know that your business needs to be found by your customer
on social media. Your business can't thrive in today's world without
having a presence there. But, how do you generate a return on your
investment of time, money and energy? How do you actually make a
profit from using social media?

In this section, I'll share the secret to selling on social media that no
one talks about. Social media is a distribution channel. Think of your
content as the sales funnel that you use on social media.

I'll examine the importance of relationship marketing and discuss the SWIIFT model in more detail because this strategy is rarely adopted in today's business world, especially not online.

Finally, I'll explain why you need social networks, how often you should use them, and which ones you should be using.

The Secret to Selling on Social Media

Everyone is trying to sell on social media but when you think about it, the truth is that it's difficult to get people to buy your products or services until they know, like, trust, and NEED what you sell.

The biggest clue in the actual phrase social media is one word, "social."

People use social media to engage in conversation, catch up with friends and family, and to follow the news, celebrities and brands they are most interested in. They aren't really using social media with the intention of buying something. They are using social media to consume content and socialize with other people.

The sales funnel I am about to share, allows you to distribute your content to people who are interested in what you do, engage with those people, generate leads for your business, and ultimately create sales opportunities.

Social media is a primary distribution channel for your content. The two work hand-in-hand in building you a successful and profitable business.

Let me explain six steps in the sales funnel strategy which incorporate content and ultimately lead to sales when using social media:

1. Awareness
2. Visibility
3. Engagement
4. Lead

5. Nurture
6. Sale

Now let's cover what each of these six steps mean.

1. Awareness

Awareness is at the top of the funnel. It is at the top of the funnel because people cannot choose you or even consider you for business if they are not aware that you exist.

Your first goal on social media is to build awareness around your business so that the right people know that you exist. Social media provides a platform where you can share your content and use social media advertising to get your business in front of the people who need your products and or services.

By being on social media, you also allow the people who already do business with you to tag you and engage with your business. This helps others to become aware of you too because when your customers engage with you, the people connected to them see that engagement and therefore see your business too.Let me give you an example you may not have considered.

Recently, I wanted to order flowers for a client of mine who is located in Miami. I don't know a local flower shop there so I had to Google Miami florist. I then proceeded to look at websites and Facebook pages until I found a florist who created designs that I liked. If they had not had a presence on social media, I wouldn't have become aware of them and their style. If they didn't post regular content allowing me to see their designs, I would not have chosen them.

2. Visibility

You become visible when your content shows up for others over and over again on social media. Think of it as being similar to bench or billboard advertising. You see the same ad repeatedly each day when you drive to and from work and over time you feel a sense of familiarity with the business on the ad. Social media works the same way.

When visibility happens repeatedly over a period of time, people start to have a perceived feeling about you and your business. That feeling is formed and solidified by the content you share and the people who engage with your content.

Oprah is a classic example of what I mean by visibility and the feeling of familiarity. The vast majority of us have not met Oprah, but we feel like we know her because she's been so visible through television, her magazine, and social media for years. We feel a sense of intimacy and trust.

The same applies to you and your business on social media. When you show up on a regular basis and share valuable content, people grow to know, like, and trust you based on that content. It makes an impact on people's perception of your business.

Keep in mind, however, that this visibility can also work where people know, dislike, and distrust you if you are not careful. What you share and say in a social media setting impacts how you make people feel about you and your brand, even when you think it is on your "private" profile. My rule of thumb is this—If you wouldn't want your mom to read it or you wouldn't want it quoted on a giant billboard, don't post it on social media.

People like to do business with people they know, like, and trust.

There are three ways you can increase your visibility on social media and earn that trust:

1. Organic reach by posting content
2. Paid reach by advertising content
3. Social reach by engaging with other people's content

All three of these allow you to gain visibility and for more people to see you on a regular basis. Remember, out of sight equals out of mind. You want to be visible so you are top of mind for others.

3. Engagement

Engagement is the third part of the sales funnel. When your content is good, people will start to engage with you and your content by liking, sharing, or commenting.

On social media this is important because every time someone interacts with a piece of content, that interaction creates a separate story to help you build additional awareness through the person who engaged with your content— your friends, family, and even the nosy neighbors who are in their circle of influence!

Let me illustrate for you: If you are on Facebook and we are friends and you like or comment on Lady Gaga's page, this may show up in my newsfeed as a piece of content or a story because I am connected to you. Because you have engaged with Lady Gaga, and I, too, like Lady Gaga, there is a higher likelihood that I may engage with her page, too.

Engagement can show up in a variety of ways.

You get engagement when someone chooses to follow or like your business, when someone likes or shares a piece of the content you post, or when someone comments or communicates with you directly via that social network.

Sometimes people engage in a negative manner, and you would be surprised at how your community may respond. A few years ago, a client of mine had someone post a nasty comment on their Facebook page. Almost immediately, other people who also liked their page started commenting and supporting my client. There was such an outpouring of support from their community that they did not need to address the negative comment.

4. Lead

Once you have developed a certain level of awareness, visibility, and engagement, you can offer someone an opportunity to take another step in getting to know your business.

I call this a lead, but really it is just a way for you to get someone to put up his or her hand and say, *"Yes, I am interested in learning more about what you offer."*

I do this by offering what I call a piece of premium content. Premium content is something that I share in exchange for an email address. One of the ways I do this is typically via paid advertising on a social network that takes the individual to a website landing page with some type of offer they can get for free in exchange for their email address.

Some of the things I have given away for free are e-books, video training, webinars, and even virtual events specifically for this purpose.

When you are creating this type of premium content, often referred to as a lead magnet, you allow people to take another step in getting to know you and your business. It is important to become good at writing sound bites that will stand out and interest your audience. The words you use in your copy, as well as the graphic you use, will influence whether someone decides to take that next step.

How do you get better at this? Practice, pilot and pay attention to what works.

Frequently, we get into the spray-and-pray mentality of marketing and fail to notice what worked really well and why something else fell flat. Pay attention to your copy and how people respond to you. See what makes people interact and what people completely avoid, and that will teach you what to do more of.

Study people who are really good at doing this and model (not copy) what they do. Most often, you will see the people who are *really good* focus on relationships, are always adding value, and share really great content.

Here's another secret—You always want to ensure that whatever you give away for free is a dynamite piece of premium content because you want people to be impressed. You want to make it so good that people will be amazed that they didn't have to pay for what you gave them. *This is something that most people fail on.*

People worry about giving good stuff away for free instead of realizing that it is the most important part of turning connections into customers. When you give freely, people trust and respect you, and then they start to talk about you. Don't skimp here.

When your connection becomes a lead, something happens. You shift the dynamic of the communication between you and them. You now appear in their email Inbox where you have more control around reaching them than you do on social media.

That lead can help you to generate sales and sales opportunities, but as I emphasized in the earlier chapter—*it all starts with your content.* It is no longer reasonable for you to have a business without regularly creating content. If you fail to create new content, your potential customers may visit your website and judge you as irrelevant.

Content is the number one way to increase awareness, visibility, and engagement. It is the catalyst that allows you to turn connections into customers. Never underestimate the value or importance of the people whose Inbox you show up in regularly. They matter.

5. Nurture

Nurturing is the fifth and most critical part of the sales funnel. Someone has now gone from being a connection on social media to being a part of your community or your list. When this happens, you want to initially segregate your connection from the rest of your community and nurture the connection via a series of emails that are designed to allow the connection to get to know you even better.

I know, you want to sell them something, but your connection *does not* want to be sold to.

If you want to turn that new lead into a paying customer, you have to spend some time and effort nurturing the relationship before you ask them to buy something. When you ask people to buy right away, it is a turn off. After all, all they did was subscribe to something you offered for free.

People love to buy, but they hate to be sold to.

When you set up a lead magnet to offer people something for free in exchange for an email address, you should also set up a series of emails designed to offer them even more value and to give them an opportunity to get to know your business better.

After you send that series of emails, you can follow up with some type of special offer, but only after you have given them extreme value. The reason this approach tends to work is because of the Law of Reciprocity. When you give someone something, they automatically want to do something nice back for you. The same thing happens when you deliver really great information to someone's inbox, if you do a great job at helping them, and then provide them an opportunity to buy, they naturally want to support you.

This is a really simple thing to do but most people won't do it because they are impatient and too eager to just sell, sell, sell. They don't care about adding value first.

When someone becomes a lead in my pipeline, I want to nurture that relationship. It's so much easier to sell when you've nurtured a relationship. You don't have to work as hard to try and "sell" because when you deliver value over and over, people end up wanting more and wanting to buy.

When you fail to nurture that relationship and leap directly to trying to close a sale, you will make people feel very uncomfortable.

They will sense that your intention is really all about making money, not about service, and they won't buy.

The better you know your audience, the easier it is to nurture them. If you know your audience is female, then you need to nurture the relationship before you ask for money. If, however, your audience is male, they might not take it personally if you want to sell to them straight away. Men (not all) are more likely to buy something when they need it, whereas women are more relationship oriented and dislike a pushy sales approach.

Once you have nurtured these relationships, they fall into your regular email communication sequence, which we discussed in the previous chapter.

My community members are used to hearing from me and getting something of value every week. So when I do invite them to a new webinar or tell them about a new book or program being launched, they are responsive because of the relationships I've built with them. Some are loyal to the point that it doesn't matter what I'm selling, they want to participate because they are fans of the results they get from working with me.

A part of the nurturing that I mentioned earlier is about being reliable. It's about being professional and being consistent. You want people to know that they can count on your to keep delivering great information designed to serve them.

Get your nurturing right, focus on delivering value and building relationships and it will be much easier to convert leads into sales.

6. Sale

The last part of the sales funnel is the sale. Once you have spent time nurturing and building a relationship with your lead, your business has a much better chance of turning that lead into a customer if they are interested in what you have to offer.

This can happen a number of different ways. Your lead may reach out to you and express an interest in your business or you may present them with an offer.

If you want to present them with an offer to buy, you can do this either via an email, a series of emails, a sales page, or during a live event such as a webinar.

When you are selling, keep in mind that typically the higher the price point, the longer the sales cycle. For example, you can convert a lead into a $7 sale pretty easily, but converting a lead into a $5,000 sale or a $25,000 sale takes more time, effort, and nurturing.

The type of offer you have will also depend on whether you have something you can sell online or if you have a brick-and-mortar establishment to which you are trying to drive foot traffic.

Once you have gained awareness, visibility, and credibility through the content you share and you engage people, the lead process starts to feel very organic. As I said earlier, people like to buy, but they don't like to feel sold to, so you'll want to develop a heightened sense of awareness around people's buying signals.

For example, when people start asking me questions in a Facebook chat about their business, I'm on high alert for buying signals right away—this person is asking me about business, *this is a potential sale.*

There is the possibility that this person is interested in working with me based on the type of questions they are asking. Therefore, I want to make them feel good in terms of how I communicate or I potentially lose the opportunity to do business with them.

It's really no different than walking into a retail store and the sales person who's working there is more interested in texting on their mobile phone than they are in helping you. You'll take your business elsewhere. People don't like being ignored.

When you log in to Facebook and ignore the person asking you about your business, they will take their business somewhere else. You need to be aware that there's an enormous amount of business taking place on social media if you just pay attention. You need to be savvy and you need to be SWIIFT (See What's In It For Them). You have to show up regularly, interact with others, engage in conversation with people, and *treat them with respect when they demonstrate any kind of interest in your business.*

Always Look for Buying Signals

There are easy ways to recognize buying signals but not everyone does.

Buying signals for me include questions like:

- Do you offer a sales training program?
- Do you offer Facebook coaching?
- Do you provide "Done for You" services?

They are asking you if you do what they are looking for.

They don't ask about Facebook training unless they're looking for Facebook training.

If someone asks me if I offer Facebook training and I only reply, "Yes, I do" and nothing more, I have lost the opportunity to further engage with the potential customer.

But, what if I reply, *"Yes, I offer many different kinds of training. We have online programs, and I offer private one-on-one coaching and a team of people who offer Facebook implementation for you—what is it that you were looking to learn about Facebook exactly?"*

In that example, what I'm doing is taking that question and *asking a question back* to keep the conversation going.

You do not want to shut people down when they ask a question. You want to take their inquiry seriously because it's a signal to say they might be interested in working with you.

Let's go back to the retail store example. If someone walks into a retail store and asks if you sell Levis, clearly they are looking for jeans so if you don't have Levis, you need to say, "We don't have Levis but we sell five other brands. Can I show you what we have?"

People fail to identify buying signals because:

- They don't have clarity on their business model.
- They're afraid to sell, which makes them afraid to engage in order to avoid hearing *"no."*
- They fear rejection. They're waiting for people to treat them like a grocery store and walk up to the checkout and say, "I want to buy this."

That is not what really happens in business!

Offer people what you have by engaging in a sales conversation whether that's face-to-face or online. It's all connected to how you communicate and make people feel about your business. You need to build relationships with your potential customers through your social networks in order to have the opportunity to serve them through your sales.

The Goal of Your Sales Funnel

It's not impossible, but it's much more difficult to generate sales through social media if you don't following the steps outlined in this chapter.

Think about how a funnel works.

The widest point on the funnel is the place when the largest numbers of people enter. As you get further into the funnel, the people who aren't interested your business go away or keep consuming your content and you're left with the people who are interested in doing business with you.

In essence, you are reducing the levels of rejection you're going to receive because you've allowed people to decide on the next step for them along the way. This means you know who is and who is not interested in your products or services and you are able to focus on those who really are interested in your business.

I look at the funnel as a process that allows people to self-select and determine whether they want to take the next step with you.

If you lead with sales at the top of the funnel, you are making it much harder because you are not giving yourself the opportunity to filter down to the most- qualified people who are interested in your business. Therefore, you are increasing your rejection rate.

For the third time, people love to buy but they hate being sold, especially on social media.

They're afraid to have conversations with people when they feel like that person is just trying to get them to buy something. A perfect example of this is Nerium International, a direct sales company that is in growth mode. No disrespect to this company, but I was inundated with private messages from people I have never had conversations with before trying to pitch me on this business. Not only is this ineffective, the approach turned me off of even wanting to be a customer of theirs. When your sales people don't understand the selling process, you put your company's reputation at risk.

This type of selling doesn't work because you haven't built a relationship and or qualified that I might be interest. Focus on the relationship first and stop trying to sell blindly to people you don't know. It will minimize rejection and maximize your sales potential. Now let's talk about which social networks you should use.

CHAPTER EIGHT

DON'T BE EVERYWHERE ON SOCIAL MEDIA

"If I observed all the rules, I'd never have got anywhere."
– Marilyn Monroe

Understanding Social Media Networks

Social media has changed the landscape of marketing and networking significantly since Facebook launched in 2004. It has levelled the playing field creating many opportunities for small and mid-sized companies that once upon a time only existed for big companies.

Today, your company's relevance is determined often by the perception your customers have of you and your social networking savvy. Are you present? Do you share? Do you engage? Are you offering value and fun ways for your customers to interact with you?

When you think about traditional advertising, it was previously a one-way form of communication. Television, print, and radio ads were designed to send a message to the customer without receiving any real feedback in return.

Social media has created a networking vehicle where you can engage with your customers and receive feedback from them in real time when you market.

You can assess how successful your message is by the response you receive from others.

Because of this, it's critical that your business has a presence on social media.

In today's technology-driven society, when someone is interested in your business they Google you. When people Google you, they want to see all of the places they can go to engage and learn more about you and your business.

Social networks allow your customer to get a glimpse of who you are personally and professionally.

If your customer cannot find you or your business on social media, then they question your relevance. You might not like hearing this, but that's the way the world is today. To dismiss the relevance of social media is like dismissing the impact television and telecommunications would have on the world many years ago.

It's time to embrace change.

Which Sites to Use

Some marketers will tell you that you should be everywhere. I believe that your choice of social networks should depend on what your business objective is. You want to spend time where your customers are and prioritize your time so that you can make a real impact on the social networks you choose.

As a professional, you may want to have a LinkedIn presence so that other professionals can find you. At this time, LinkedIn is perceived in the professional world as the most credible social network for business. If your customer is a business owner, CEO, or even a manager of a corporation, this will likely be the best place to connect with them.

Facebook is the most popular social media network in many parts of the world so you will want a presence there, too. If your customer is a consumer or a small business owner, you will probably find them on Facebook sharing photos and information with friends and family and connecting to brands they know, like, and trust. Large companies and brands use Facebook because they know they can reach the consumers of their products and services easily through Facebook's robust advertising platform.

Twitter is like a big networking party where you can access anyone, anywhere. You can have quick conversations with people and follow anyone or any topic you want because most of the platform is for sharing, conversing and communicating public updates. Twitter search is a powerful tool for listening and connecting with people who are talking about things that align with what you do.

On your Facebook profile, you require permission to be friends with someone and you have multiple options around who sees the content you share from public to extremely private. Facebook also allows you to enable a follower option if you wish to share public updates, however, they limit your friend count to just 5,000. Alternatively, on Twitter you have no limit to the number of followers you can have.

YouTube is one social resource that many businesses overlook. It allows you to share video content so that people can see and feel the message you want to share. This is as close to being in person as you can get on social media and very few people use this social network to connect and engage with other users.

Video used to be harder to get to the masses but with the changes in cellular download speeds, video is being consumed on mobile devices at a faster rate than ever before. People can *see and feel* your energy through video and for a prospective new customer there is huge value in using this medium to market your business.

While it may be important to use all of these social networks, you don't need to use all of them all of the time. There are new social networks popping up constantly and for many people there is an undercurrent of fear that makes you feel like if you don't jump on Instagram, Pinterest, Google+, and Periscope that you may get left behind.

Don't succumb to this unless you want to be everywhere and have time to do it all. It is better to use one or two social networks and do a really good job engaging, sharing, and building your community than it is to spread yourself thin by being on 10 different networks that you don't have time to use.

If you love Facebook and only occasionally use Twitter, put on your Twitter bio that you use Twitter once in a while and provide the link there to your Facebook page for those who want to connect.

People think they have to be everywhere, but I disagree. I would suggest you pick the social networks that are most relevant for you and your business. If this was 1990, and you were a small business owner, you wouldn't be doing national and local newspaper ads, plus national and local radio ads, plus television commercials on every network because your budget would not allow for it. Social media may not require the same financial commitment but it does require time or resources, so choose accordingly.

You also want to look at the demographics of each social network, compare them to your business and ideal customer, and decide what makes sense. For example, if you're a photographer and you photograph a lot of weddings, you need to be on Pinterest and Instagram because brides frequently look at wedding-related photography prior to getting married. Brides typically are a younger demographic and statistics show that they are using Instagram more than Facebook and that they all use Pinterest to store wedding inspiration ideas.

Know your customer. Know where they hang out. Know how they engage on social media so that your business can be there to serve and engage with them. And, as much as possible, know which social networks are referring traffic and leads to your website. You can get this information from Google Analytics.

As a business owner, understand what social networks support your business the best and spend your time there. It all comes back to knowing who your customer is and where your customer spends their time.

A couple great books that talk about all of the social networks and their differences in more detail are *The Art of Social Media* by Guy Kawasaki or *Jab, Jab, Jab, Right Hook* by Gary Vaynerchuk. It's a good idea to read books like these so that you understand more about posting your content the right way on each of these platforms because they are not all the same. One mistake people make regularly is to use a social media scheduling tool like HootSuite and post or schedule the same content everywhere, and one thing Gary's book shows you is why this does not always work.

Re-evaluate Regularly

As part of your business strategy, I would encourage you to evaluate and re-evaluate the social networks you use on a regular basis so that you can discern which ones are the best for you. Ask the following questions:

- Which ones are generating the best return for your business?
- Which ones are allowing you to receive referrals?
- Which ones are helping you to distribute your content and reach a larger audience?

It is important that you *choose* where and whether you show up on social networks. Don't avoid social media because you don't understand how it can work for your business. Learn, because social networks are not going away any time soon.

The benefits I see for each network at the time of writing this book.

Facebook

Facebook is the social networking site where most of my customers hang out. The benefits of having a profile, a business page and a group on Facebook are endless and I could probably write an entire book about why I use Facebook. For the purpose of this chapter, however, I will just discuss some of my favorites.

The biggest plus around using Facebook is their advertising platform. You can advertise to a group of people based on geography and interests and you can do some really targeted ads using Facebook Power Editor.

The Facebook advertising platform gives you so much control over your advertising that it can be overwhelming, but don't let that discourage you. Facebook ads allow you to:

- Place a piece of code on your website and then advertise to anyone who has visited your website.
- Upload a list of email addresses and create a custom audience based on email addresses found on Facebook and advertise to that group of people.
- Create a lookalike audience based on the demographics of your custom audience or even based on the likes of another business page on Facebook.

It may sound complicated but the opportunities are endless for business owners, and you also are in complete control of your budget.

You can advertise to a specific and targeted audience for as little as a dollar a day.

The other reason I like Facebook is that it is a recognizable social network. I can use a Facebook Like button or Like Box on my website and most people are comfortable and familiar with how to use them. I can choose the level of access I want to give people by accepting them as friends, converting them to followers, or referring them to my business page. You also get a lot of control and flexibility around the audience you share your content with.

LinkedIn

LinkedIn allows you to set up a professional profile and a business page. It also has a publishing platform that you can use on your profile to distribute your content much like a blog only it is housed within LinkedIn rather than on your website. The value of using LinkedIn's publishing platform is that your content gets indexed on LinkedIn and if LinkedIn Pulse picks up your published content it can have a viral impact very quickly if the content is good.

LinkedIn also allows you to post and receive written recommendations. These recommendations can add credibility around the work you do. It allows others to see people who have done business with you and the value they received from you when they are legitimate recommendations.

Twitter

Twitter used to be one of my favorite social networks. However, in recent months I have found that the level of engagement on Twitter has significantly declined and that many people use Twitter only to automate marketing messages. It's a prime example of too many people doing the wrong thing causing the platform to lose credibility as a professional resource.

Don't misunderstand. I don't believe that Twitter is "dead." I like the value of relationship marketing and believe there is a big opportunity on Twitter right now for someone who is dedicated to following keywords to really build relationships and their business through this channel.

My favorite things about Twitter are brevity (you can only post 140 characters), lists, and keyword searches.

Many people are concerned with the number of followers they have. Don't be. Be more concerned with building relationships, the topics you want to talk to people about and the capability of sorting people into relevant lists so that you can review content and communicate with them based on those lists.

For example, if you were marketing to Real Estate Agents, you could set up a list for just them and really hone in on having conversations with that group of people without ever following any of them.

You can do the same thing by using topics, or hashtags. I like to follow hashtags in the city I live in, and I like to also list all my clients in a private list so that I can be SWIIFT about how I engage with them.

There is a lot of noise on Twitter. Saved searches and lists allow you to fine-tune what you want to consume and whom you want to engage with.

Pinterest

If you share blog content with great visuals or if you are a retailer who sells products and services online, Pinterest could be one of your top traffic drivers.

Pinterest is a visual storyboard where your images and copy come together, creating a unique way for you to engage with your audience. When you share content on Pinterest, whether it is free content or items people can buy, you will quickly find that Pinterest becomes a huge referral site for your website.

If you sell actual retail goods, having a Pinterest account, high-quality images, appropriate keywords, and catchy copy is a must.

Google+

Google controls search online. Therefore, it stands to reason that having a Google+ profile or business page makes sense. While I am not a daily user of this social networking site, I do see its value.

What I like the most about this site is how what you share on Google+ affects your SEO. If I am logged into Google+ and I Google something, I can see that preferential treatment is given to people I am connected to in my search results.

I am also a huge fan of Google Hangouts as a way to connect real time with people. Google Hangouts allows you to hang out with up to nine other people or you can live stream to a larger audience. I love this functionality and I have used Google Hangouts as a replacement for webinars. My team uses Google Hangouts almost daily as a virtual in-person touch point.

YouTube

YouTube is the second most popular search engine on the web and is owned by Google. People want "how-to" videos to answer the questions they type into Google. Video should be an important part of your marketing mix if you are an author/speaker/coach or if you have a business where you want to demonstrate how to do something or how to use a product.

Video is a great way to create content if you don't like to write but you're good at speaking. You can use YouTube as a substitute for blogging by taking your YouTube videos and embedding them into your blog as content. Another great way to leverage your video content is to produce a video and then get someone to transcribe it and post the content on your blog or use it to create a different blog later on.

Podcasts

If you like speaking but you don't like the way you look on video (trust me, nobody does), you can instead produce a Podcast. Podcasts are incredibly popular and will continue to gain in popularity. Car manufacturers are now integrating the ability for you to listen to podcasts into your car, which will make them even more popular than they are right now.

So, what is a Podcast? A Podcast is an audio recording you produce and upload as a show for people to listen to when they want. A Podcast is like radio on demand. You can also do video Podcasts but for the purpose of this section, I am referring to the audio format.

If you are creating a Podcast, a smart way to maximize this piece of content is to upload your podcast and then have a URL where you can send your audience to get more information or to download a transcription. Your Podcast could become a way to share premium content and add more people to the community, lovingly referred to as your list. I will share my favorite business podcasts in the resources download you receive with this book which you can find at www. PilotToProfit.com/FreeTools.

How Much Time Does Social Media Take?

This should be decided based on your business needs, but there are a few rules of thumb you can follow:

1. Carve out time every day to show up, share, and engage on social media. There is no magical amount of time that you should spend each day. Spend what you can, focus on quality versus quantity, and make an effort to show up daily.

2. It is better to spend 15 minutes sharing great content and engaging with others than 1 hour a day mindlessly surfing newsfeeds. It's easy to get lost in a newsfeed and caught up in

what others are doing when you don't have a clear plan of how you want social media to work for you.

3. Don't use social media as a way to procrastinate and avoid work and then blame social media for not generating leads for your business.

If I'm bored and I log into Facebook and scroll mindlessly, that's procrastinating. That's wasting time versus logging into LinkedIn, deliberately reaching out to three people I'd like to do business with, and/ or publishing a new piece of content that lets people know about my thought leadership.

One is intentional; one is mindless. You get to choose which you do.

What's SWIIFT?

When you are SWIIFT, you *See What's In It For Them*. See What's In It For Them means you are constantly looking to see how you can serve, support, share, and engage with others.

When you operate from a place of WIIFM, your orientation is What's In It For Me. That's what most people do on social media. They focus on, *"How many likes, comments, friends, and followers can I get?"*

WIIFM is the complete opposite of being SWIIFT. Most people are operating from a place of What's In It For Me. You can completely stand out from the crowd when you See What's In It For Them.

There's a big difference between being intentional on social media and being mindless. If you use social media the same way a couch potato watches TV, that's not intentional. That's mindless.

We all have our biases, filters, likes, and dislikes. That is why I believe the content you share on your social networks should match the strategy of your business and encompass SWIIFT.

People use social media without having clarity on their overarching business strategy, and sadly in some cases that is because they have no real business strategy. Therefore, they employ spray-and-pray marketing tactics on social media that are guaranteed to fail and often are narcissistic or WIIFM-oriented.

Social media is a tactic that allows you to connect with other people to execute your business strategy. Social media should help you to gain more awareness and visibility for your business and help you to build connections with others. If you are a skilled social networker, and you are SWIIFT, you can turn those connections into paying customers. That's why relationship marketing is such an important part of building your business.

CHAPTER NINE
BE A SWIIFT MARKETER

"Too often, feeling intimidated becomes our excuse not to be awesome."
– Scott Stratten

Relationship marketing is exactly what it sounds like.

I t is about building a relationship with people who have an interest in your products and or services and paving the way for them to select your business as the one they choose to do business with.

When you build relationships with people, see how you can help them, and demonstrate credibility in everything you do, you get results. When you do this regularly, sales start to take care of themselves because people are attracted to you not just because of what you sell but also because of who you are.

Relationships help you grow your business.

One way to do this is to create great content that has value and is useful for people.

The other way is to focus on getting to know people.

Those two things are key to the growth of your business.

More About Being SWIIFT

When you See What's In It For Them, you are being SWIIFT.

SWIIFT is about building relationships with your ideal client through your social network. It's a mindset about seeing how you can serve and build relationships with others.

Everyone logs into their social media accounts to check their personal notifications, messages, and friend requests because that's all about them. They want to know:

- Who commented on what I posted?
- Who sent me a message?
- Who wants to be my friend?

It doesn't matter what social network it is, you don't log in primarily to see what everyone else is doing. You log in and the first thing you do is to see what's happening for you.

When you log in and are SWIIFT, you make it first about others, not you.

When you share content on social media, be mindful and share something of value that can help someone else. Comment, like, and show up in other peoples' space on a regular basis so that they know you see them and notice what they are doing.

If someone comments on a post of yours, respond. Let people know you see them.

Every time you like, comment, or engage with others on social media it shows up as a notification for the other person. If you want to build relationships, you need to start from the frame of reference of being SWIIFT.

To adopt the SWIIFT approach you need to ask yourself:

- Am I giving or am I taking?
- Is this serving me or is this serving others?
- Is this about my own personal significance or ego, or is it about contribution?

The answer to these questions will help you to understand if you are being SWIIFT.

Let's look at an example.

I have a blog post that explains how to deal with Facebook imposters, who are people who take your account name and send friend requests out to people who are already your friends. It leads to confusion.

I kept getting all of these friend requests from people who I was already friends with, so I took a look and could see right away that someone had impersonated their account. When I looked a little closer, I was amazed at how many people were accepting the request without actually realizing this was an imposter. I wrote a blog post explaining the steps to deal with this issue.

Now, whenever I see that it's happened to someone else, I share the blog post. This post has been liked on Facebook hundreds of times because it's been that useful for others. All I do is share it, I don't ask people to like and share it, however, I look for people who need help and I offer it as a way to serve them.

See What's in It for Them

When you are SWIIFT, you are doing the exact opposite of what everyone else is doing on social media. This tactic alone will enable you to gain engagement. Yes, it requires time, energy, effort, and thought to produce content and be this engaging, helpful, and useful for others— *but it works.*

Here's another tip.

With all of my private coaching clients on Facebook, I star them as a close friend and enable notifications to be sent to me for everything they do because it allows me to pay close attention to their activity. That, in turn, allows me to be present and support them. I don't leave it to chance. I put processes in place to ensure I know what is going on with these individuals because they are important to me.

If you're working on a deal with someone and they are a lead, the smart thing to do is to pay attention to what they're doing and look for opportunities to engage and build the relationship, too. I'm not saying you have to like and comment on every single thing they post, but they should be on your radar. That's just a smart business practice because if you leave it up to the social network to show you what's going on, you may never know.

Ultimately, you get to choose the people you build relationships with, you don't have to sit back and wait for them to come to you.

The best way to gain a friend is to be a friend.

The best way to gain a customer is to serve others as often as you can.

Showing Up

What I've just described with the example from Facebook is about showing up.

Let's face it, social media experts are a dime a dozen. Why do people come to me for help with social media?

It's because I show up regularly, engage with others regularly, create content, and add value all the time. I've built credibility through the work I have done with other people. That's a whole bunch of little things that add up to something big over time.

Showing up means paying attention to what people are viewing, and analyzing the nuances of what they're saying and not saying.

Showing up means being in tune with when you should offer encouragement or support or a helping hand.

Showing up means being authentic, not manipulative.

Let me give you an example.

I have a client who does work in the grief and loss area. She had been posting content on Facebook to really try and help people. She comes from a vulnerable spot in how she's showing up, and I know that she worries about what people think. Recently, I sent her a message to acknowledge how she's been showing up. I told her, "I see what you're doing, I love what you're doing, and you're making a difference."

Here's another example.

I had a call with a client recently and she sounded really down so I sent her a message later to say, "I just want to check in and make sure you're okay because you sounded really down earlier. It could be you're really busy at work, it could be something personal, or it could be my team or I are doing something you're upset about and you didn't want to bring it up on the call. However, I wanted to check in to see if there's anything wrong that I can fix or anything going on I can help with."

She replied saying, "I'm busy at work but it's nothing I can't handle." I wanted to support her so the next thing I did was send an email to my florist asking her to send this client some flowers because I could tell in her voice that she was having a bad day and could use some appreciation.

In both examples *I offered encouragement*—that missing ingredient in the lives of most people.

It's easy to do and it's especially helpful with business owners because they don't have anyone to tell them they're doing a good job—but there's more to showing up than that.

Show up regularly and you notice what's going on with others.

While speaking at an event, someone asked to talk to me about a new network marketing product line they were bringing into Canada. They were looking for a way to connect with distributers in a new market and thought I might have some suggestions on how to do this via social media.

I knew someone who worked in this space who was looking for something new so I offered to reach out and introduce them via Facebook.

The person who asked for my help didn't log into Facebook daily so after I spoke to my contact, verified her interest, and made the initial introduction 3 or 4 days passed. During that same window of time, someone else approached her and the other person lost the opportunity to have this person help her bring her business to Canada.

Showing up means monitoring and responding to your messages on social media.

People express interest in working with me via messages on Facebook almost daily.

I always respond to these messages promptly unless they are spam or someone is trying to sell me something and I don't know who they are.

Consider social media as an extension of your regular email Inbox.

Treat your notifications and messages on social media with the same urgency as regular email and voicemail. It is just another access point for people who are interested in doing business with you.

If you are using social media for your business, it needs to become a part of your business practice to check in.

Many people don't do this because they're too focused on "What's In It For Me" rather than on being SWIIFT.

When your mindset is SWIIFT, you'll always do things to surprise and delight the people you want to do business with.

Know Your Customer

One final point to make in closing this chapter is that you have to know who your customer is in order to be successful on social media.

Some people think everyone is their customer. Everyone can be, but not everyone will be. Some things you may want to consider are:

- Who is the ideal customer you love to do business with?
- Where can you go to build relationships with those people who represent your ideal customer?
- How can you train yourself to recognize your ideal customer when you meet them?

The majority of my customers are women who are between the ages of 45 and 65. Their kids are no longer at home and this is a time in their life to focus on themselves. These women are smart, savvy business owners and they know what they don't know and are not afraid to seek out help to support the vision they have for their business.

They invest in themselves regularly, care about their customers, and find meaning in their work.

They want to know how to grow their business, leverage social media, and use technology to get results. They want to hire someone to help them because they want to be independent and not seek help from their kids. Many of these women have had different life careers and this is the first business venture they've had on their own.

Knowing this about my customers means that when they are in front of me I can easily recognize who my customer is. I have a heightened sense of awareness when I am interacting with this woman so that she feels heard and validated in the work she is doing.

There will always be exceptions to this. I have worked with women in their 20s and 30s and I also work with men, but that's not the norm.

I know who the majority of my customer base is and I know what the exceptions are. When you focus on the majority versus always searching for the exception, you can grow your business faster.

In order for your efforts to be successful and for you to achieve results faster than average, know who your customer is. Most people never take the time to do this work and it is one of the key reasons they struggle to grow their business and create real long-term profits and success.

SECTION 4
SELLING PRINCIPLES

Chapter Ten

How To Sell

"There is no rule that says everyone has to buy from you equally."
– Colleen Francis

K nowing and building relationships is key, but knowing how to
sell once you get those potential customers in front of you is
just as, if not more, important.

Selling Is a Skill

Nothing happens in business until someone buys something and in
order for someone to buy.... you have to sell or at least close the sale.
Many business owners don't know how to sell and the thought of selling
makes them very uncomfortable. They don't know how to sell because
they have never learned how and in many cases, they are afraid and have
limiting beliefs around what it means to sell.

Selling is a skill. It is something you can learn to do from a place of
honor and authenticity.

Selling is a skill that relies on your communication, listening, and problem-solving abilities. In order for your business to grow and prosper, selling is necessary.

There is no point in doing everything you can to market and send people to your website and your business if there isn't anyone who can sell to them once they get there.

The great news is, because selling is a skill, it is something that you can learn.

Some people are born with natural sales abilities. They are charismatic and good at asking the right questions and listening to people. Some parts may come more naturally to some people than others; however, all parts are learnable.

In the first chapter, I told you my story about selling items at the age of 12 when I wanted a pair of designer jeans that my mom could not afford to buy. When I brought my things to the flea market and I sold what I had, I was not skilled.

I didn't know enough to consider that I was "selling" but I had a desire that made me very motivated to succeed. The skill I have now when it comes to selling is much more sophisticated than it was when I was 12 years old, but the desire is still strong.

The one thing I could do easily, even at the age of 12, was talk to people. When you can strike up a conversation easily with a stranger and build a rapport, it is the gateway to allowing you to sell your products and services.

You can build your confidence and competence around selling when you go through structured training, learn a certain methodology, and learn how to approach selling.

You might be reading this now and thinking. *'That's never going to be me. I can't sell and the thought of it scares me. It fills me with a sense of fear.'* But you can, and the reason I know you can is this:

Having trained hundreds, if not thousands, of people in retail to sell, I have measured their ability to sell prior to training and again after they completed their training. When they improve their skill level, they become effective at selling—*and that means you can too.*

In The Sales Pilot, I've created a framework to train, coach, and support business owners on learning how to sell. We focus on the skill-based things they can do, and these business owners have been able to make significant strides in their sales. Some have closed their largest sale ever because of this training and others have had their highest month in sales in the history of their business. It doesn't matter where you start; we celebrate everyone's progress in learning and increasing sales.

When it comes to selling and business, you really don't know what you don't know, until you know.

If you don't know what the structure of a sales process looks like, then you'll always struggle to sell because you probably think selling is telling—and it isn't.

Selling is asking, listening, solving, and helping someone make a buying decision. Selling comes from understanding and solving someone's needs. Selling is an act of service when done well.

This is what selling looks like:

- Building a rapport with a potential customer so they feel comfortable around you.
- Inquiring as to what their needs are so you understand exactly what it is they are looking for and how to serve them.
- Presenting solutions that meet those needs.
- Overcoming and anticipating objections they might have to what you offer them.
- Asking and answering questions around the objections they have to buying.

- Closing the sale by asking them to decide if what you have suggested is a good fit for them.

Selling is not telling.

Telling is dumping information on someone without listening or letting him or her get a word in. It's overwhelming people with "stuff" they don't need. It's all about you instead of about them. Even in selling, SWIIFT is applicable!

Let me give you a couple of examples.

Let's say you visit a car dealership (and I'm not saying all car dealerships are like this because they are not). You walk onto the lot to look at a car and the next thing you know, a sales rep strolls over and doesn't say, "Hello." Instead, he or she starts *telling* you without any pauses or breaths:

"That car has GPS, cruise control, heated seats, satellite radio, a CD player, connection for your iPhone, and a 78-month payment plan, which means if you buy it today you can take it home for $237 per month and by the way we have it in red, black, and white."

This is a classic example of telling instead of selling. Information is being thrown at you without any knowledge of what your needs are.

Another example you might be able to relate to is when you go computer shopping. The kid in the store is so excited that he starts talking to you about RAM, gaming, terabytes and hard drives, dual processors, and other terms that you don't even get. All you want to do is access email and the Internet!

All this does to a potential customer is make them feel overwhelmed and uncertain about their desire to buy. Instead of selling, this is repelling your customers and making them not want to buy and the purpose of this chapter is to show you how not to do that.

Selling is serving or solving a need.

How to Sell

Selling is transference of belief, and it is also a skill that you can master. It is really not about you, it is about *someone else feeling* that your product or service can solve a problem or need that they have.

If you want your business to be successful, you have to be okay with selling. Your company cannot succeed without salesmanship.

That doesn't mean you won't get butterflies in your belly and/or feel uncomfortable at times—that is normal. I still feel uneasy at times when I am selling.

If you think that the uncomfortable feeling of selling will go away, it may not. I've been selling since the age of 12. At times I am super-confident and other times I feel insecure about the process.

You'll find yourself at different places on the continuum of comfort when it comes to selling and in order to move towards feeling more confident, you'll want to gain competence around how to sell and what a sales cycle looks like.

You will be able to develop stronger skills around how you show up and behave in the sales and that will build your confidence. That confidence will help you close more sales and generate better results in your company.

Depending on your type of business, you may not think about selling every day. The truth is you are selling all the time. That last social media post, you tried to sell an idea. That honey-do list, you tried to sell your husband or wife on doing something for you. Selling is a natural part of your day-to-day interactions with others. The only difference is when it is for your business, money is involved.

One thing for you to consider is whether your business is transactional or relational. If it's transactional you may be selling every day. If it's relational, you may be selling a different way just to get new leads into your pipeline every day, and you will close sales only from time to time.

Most business owners have never had any type of formal sales training.

They don't understand the sales cycle, and they don't do things to increase traffic or create appointments and sales. Ultimately, they go through a "feast or famine" period in their business because they lack control around how to actually GENERATE sales.

As the owner of the company, you are responsible for selling the value of your company and helping your customer to make a buying decision.

Before we get into the system of selling, I want to talk a bit about your mindset. You may feel like following a system seems inauthentic when it comes to selling. I want you to challenge that mindset.

What if you wanted to create your own system for driving instead of following the road? You could get in your car and take your own path, but you might cause some damage to your car and destruction along the way if you didn't follow the road system that already exists, right?

Having said that, when you use your car's GPS navigation system, it doesn't always calculate the route the way that you want and you might decide to go a different way to reach your destination. But, you still follow the same core road system and arrive at your destination safely.

You can do this because you have skill—driving is a skill.

When you think about selling and following the system that I will share, follow the system until you have learned the skill. Once you have acquired the skill, you can adapt the system so that it feels good to you, keeping the core fundamentals intact.

If you got in your car and you didn't know how to drive to your destination, you would follow the system created for you via your GPS navigation. When you are more skilled and know the lay of the land, you may make different choices based on your experience and knowledge.

Selling is the same.

When you are selling, you are helping someone make a buying decision. You are not trying to force them to buy or to sell someone something they don't need.

When someone comes to me looking for a strategy session to build a solid marketing plan for their business, I don't try and sell them "Done for You" marketing services because that's not what they are looking for.

Selling is about your customer's needs.

I'll give you a few more examples.

We were interviewing designers to help us create the building plans for our new house. In one case, we started to tell the person about some of the things we wanted in our home. We had already picked out the hardwood for the floor and we were talking about what we had chosen. Suddenly, they interrupted us mid-sentence and said, "I don't really like that. I think you should go with this type of floor instead."

By focusing on what they wanted, instead of what we wanted, they made the sales process awkward. Their idea may have been better but the manner in which it was delivered made us wonder if they would be agreeable to our ideas on the entire project should we hire the person.

We decided to work with someone else because *it's not about what they like, it's about what my husband and I want and that's what sales people often forget.*

Selling is 100% about what your customer wants and needs. It's not about your agenda. When you start looking for ways to help others get what they want, selling becomes easy because all you're doing is listening to what their needs are and solving the problem.

Zig Ziglar said, "You can have everything in life you want, if you will just help enough other people get what they want."

I visited Europe in the summer of 2014 and before I left I went to Henry's, a photography store. I needed a battery charger for my camera and I wanted a little tiny camera for my trip because I didn't really want to be carrying my big camera around Europe with me.

I was looking at this tiny white Nikon camera and asked the sales guy to tell me about this camera for my trip to Europe. I told him that I wanted something that wasn't heavy and didn't scream 'tourist'.

Right away he said, "You know this Nikon camera looks small, but it's actually really heavy. Can I show you this one and another one you might like?" Then he brings out the original camera I had chosen plus another one. He then hands them both to me and gets me to feel the difference in weight. He then asked if we would be taking a lot of pictures from a distance and demonstrated the quality of an 18-megapixel camera with a 20x zoom over the original camera I had selected.

This guy sold me instantly because he was linking all of my needs to the camera and my trip to Europe. It met all three of the needs I had: it was lightweight, small enough to carry in my pocket, and it took amazing shots from a distance.

What he didn't do was get into all of the nitty gritty technical details about shutter speed, settings, video, etc. He also didn't dismiss my first choice. He handed me what I wanted and gave me a second option. He kept the conversation strictly within the confines of talking about what I wanted, and he made it easy for me to buy.

You can complicate the sales process when you go into telling mode and when you project what your preferences are onto the customer. Remember, selling isn't telling.

Selling should always be tied to your customer's need.

The way you uncover needs is by asking questions. However, even if you ask the right questions and then you don't know what to tell your customer, you could end up telling them everything and anything to try and make something stick. When you do this, it demonstrates a complete lack of skill.

So let's get into how you should approach a sale.

A Basic System for Selling

A basic system for selling is not complicated, it's easy to remember and it works. You can definitely get into a much more complex way of selling and there are TONS of great books out there on the topic, but for someone who has never had any sales training, this will get you started in developing your skill level.

1. Build a rapport by being friendly and approachable.
2. Determine needs by asking open- and closed-ended questions.
3. Offer a solution that meets the needs you uncover.
4. Overcome and anticipate buying objections.
5. Close the sale.
6. Add on other products or services that may go along with the primary purchase.

This is just a basic outline for you to familiarize yourself with the steps.

Next, we will go through each one in more detail and I will share some suggestions that you can take away to practice the skill on your own when you are interacting with your customers.

How to Build a Rapport

The most important thing you can do is connect and build a rapport with your customer. Building a rapport with a customer is the cornerstone to success in sales. When you make your customer feel welcome and comfortable around you, they feel confident about doing business with you.

This is the most important part of starting *any sales conversation*. Your ability to acknowledge people, build a rapport with them, and make them comfortable talking to you is what leads to them liking and trusting you. They'll decide whether they're going to buy from you in the first few moments of interacting with you. If you immediately turn them off by making them feel like you're not present or interested in them, you'll lose the sale before you have even begun.

Remember, people buy from people they know, like, and trust.

Think about what happens when you walk into a retail store. If you get a bad vibe or a negative attitude from the sales rep working in the store, it is likely you will leave without buying.

An easy way to build a rapport is to engage in friendly conversation back and forth with your customers. You can talk about things like the weather, what they're wearing, anything that doesn't directly relate to trying to sell to them. Your goal is to make them feel comfortable with you.

Imagine you invited someone to your home instead of your business. When he or she arrives at your home, you welcome the visitor, offer him or her something to drink, a place to sit down, and you do everything you can to make the visitor feel comfortable. You take an active interest and you play the role of being a gracious host.

When someone interacts with your business, do you go to the same effort to make him or her feel welcome and comfortable? If not, it may be costing you business.

There are many ways to build a rapport, and here are some suggestions:

- Take the initiative to be friendly first, even if you are shy.
- Look for things you might have in common with the other person.
- Practice conversation starters using things like sports, the weather, current events, etc.

When you do this in person, it's really easy. You can pay attention to things like the person's body language, what they are wearing, or anything they might have with them (kids, pets, or shopping bags).

When you are interacting over the phone, it's a bit tougher, but not impossible. Pay attention to the tone of your voice and their voice and smile while you are talking to them. As crazy as it sounds, if you look annoyed by the fact that you just had to stop what you are doing to answer the phone, they will pick up that vibe in the tone of your voice.

Also, try not to multitask when you are on the phone. People can sense if you are fully present or distracted during a conversation.

When you receive emails, you can also build a rapport in how you respond. My favorite way to do this is by asking a couple of questions to gather additional information before I respond to the initial question.

The first step in the sales process is to build a rapport and to have your potential (or existing) customer enjoy interacting with you. You want to break down whatever barrier exists between you and him/her if you want this person to be your customer.

When someone is not immediately friendly, this is a test for you. How skilled are you at winning over people who are resistant to being sold? If you cannot break down the barrier, make them comfortable around you, and get them to trust you, then you have very little chance of closing the sale.

I remember one time a guy named Dan came into my retail store. He was all worked up about a problem he had with his phone and he communicated that to me in a pretty strong manner. I attempted to talk to him about the problem then he said, *"Yes, but you are a Corporate Store!"*

What he meant was that he thought the big corporation owned my store and that I did not personally care about him because I was "just an employee" representing the big, bad corporation. The moment

I told him that I was the owner of the business, his entire demeanour completely changed towards me.

He and his entire family became customers and, for as long as I owned the store, he referred us business. Not only did he refer business, he personally brought people into our store and endorsed us. As a business owner, you want to *listen* and pick up on what might be causing the resistance to building a rapport and find a way to overcome it.

Try not to take it personally when someone is not pleasant with you. It is really not about you. When someone is grumpy towards you, usually it is because he or she has something going on in his or her own personal life or has had a bad experience before with someone in the same industry as you, which has caused him or her to be apprehensive.

Your role is to learn how to adapt to these situations and turn them around.

The majority of people you interact with will be pleasant and it will be easy to do.

The exception is often worth the extra effort because when you win someone over who is a skeptic, he or she can be the biggest referral source you NEVER expected.

If you haven't read: *How to Win Friends and Influence People* by Dale Carnegie. It is one of those classic books that will help you to master this skill even more.

How to Determine Needs

Once you've built a rapport and the person is comfortable talking with you, the next stage of the sales process is to determine what his or her needs are. You can create some type of a transition statement (just for you) that allows you to know that you are moving into the next stage of the sales process. Think of it as a psychological shift for you. At some point in the conversation, it is your responsibility to turn things over to business; after all, he or she is at your business for a reason.

There should be no disruption to the vibe of the conversation when you transition to asking questions in order to determine needs. Keeping your rapport strong throughout the sales process is important.

When I owned my store, I always used the same transition statement to move further into the sale:

"So, what brought you by the store today?"

As soon as I asked that one question, I shifted from the first step of building a rapport to the second step of determining needs. Once you do this, you can start asking questions to uncover why he or she is there, what they are looking for, and figure out how you can solve his or her problems.

Don't get caught up in what the perfect transition statement is. And, if you don't want to use one, that's okay, too. I found it is a subtle signal that also lets the customer know I am ready to move into the mode of serving their needs.

Remember this: In any sales conversation, the person asking the questions is the person in control of the sale. If your customer is asking all the questions, he or she is in control. If you are playing the role of the answer person, you have given away your power and you need to get it back.

Gaining back control is easy. You just need to ask a question, and one of the best ways to do this is to respond to a question with a question.

Let me show you a couple examples.

Example One:

Prospect: "Can you tell me what your fees are for social media strategy?"

Me: "That's a great question, and I am happy to explain that to you. Can you tell me a bit more about the type of strategy you are looking to create?"

Example Two:

Prospect: "Do you think we could meet for coffee? I'd love to learn more about what you do and how you might be able to help me."

Me: "Can you tell me a bit more about what it is you would like to learn?"

Just because someone asks you a question, does not mean you have to answer the question. Learning how to turn a question into a question is a skill and it takes practice.

The reason you want to be the one asking the questions is not to create a power struggle. It is because the more you know about your customer's needs, the easier it is for you to serve them. You have to ask questions in order to be able to offer a product or service that meets your customer's needs.

Selling is about gathering as much information as you can to help your customer make a buying decision. The more complex the sale, the more questions you will probably need to ask.

You will want to ask a variety of both open- and closed-ended questions. An open-ended question is one that does not have a closed, yes or no answer.

Here are some examples:

Open-ended question: Tell me what things are important to you in shopping for a new home?

Closed-ended questions: Do you need a garage? How many bedrooms do you want?

Open-ended questions allow your prospect to give you general information. Closed-ended questions help you drill down to specific detail once you have some of the general information around what this person needs.

The problem with only asking closed-ended questions is that you receive a lot of one-word answers, miss out on the emotion and the why behind your customers' needs, and it ends up taking a lot longer to uncover all the needs.

People typically buy for two reasons: to solve a problem and/or to fulfill an emotional desire.

Depending on the problem or need, they may be looking for a transactional or relational solution.

Are you clear on whether your customer is expecting a transaction-based purchase or a relationship-based purchase? Determining needs helps you to understand more about this and more around who, what, where, when, why, and how.

Don't underestimate the power of knowing the answers to those questions. The more you understand your customer's needs, the easier it is for you to close the sale.

Ask as many questions as you need to be able to successfully solve the problem. Otherwise, when you are met with buying objections, you will need to revisit questions you forgot to ask if you hope to overcome those objections and close the sale.

How to Offer a Solution That Meets the Needs You Uncover

Once you have gathered enough information to be able to make a suggestion on a product or service for your client, you will want to take one more critical step. This can make or break the deal.

Paraphrase back to your customer to ensure you understand his or her needs. Then, ask, *"Does that capture everything that you need?"*

This last question is key because there may be one additional piece of information that changes everything that you do not know.

I write down the things my customers say to me, and the reason I do this is because I want to acknowledge them by paraphrasing back to them exactly what I've heard.

For example, I might say to my client:

"So, based on what you've told me you are interested in marketing your business online, you want to learn how to build your list, you want to get more comfortable with creating content on a regular basis, and you want to increase your sales by 20%. Is there anything else you would like to get out of this coaching relationship or does that pretty much cover it all?"

I'm acknowledging them by demonstrating that I'm listening and asking them another question to see if there's anything else that I may have missed.

It is rare to interact with a skilled sales person and your customers will be grateful for the experience.

In many businesses today, customers are treated poorly. No one builds a rapport with them, no one asks questions, and no one seems to care. In some cases, customers aren't even acknowledged.

This is why so many customers are resistant to you—they are used to being sold to in a very poor and unskilled manner.

Once you paraphrase their needs and you are sure that you have not missed anything important, you are ready to offer them a solution. When you paraphrase back to your customer, you make them *feel* like they are *important and matter*. You have demonstrated active listening. When was the last time someone did that for you when you were shopping?

When you offer a solution, be sure to show your customer exactly how the solution meets their needs. Use their words to repeat back to them what they are looking for in the sales presentation. When you are presenting your product or service, it is a good idea to talk about what it is, how it aligns with their needs, what the benefits are, and what the cost is.

I like to always present two options. The reason I do this is that it makes it easier to transition to a trial close by asking them which one they prefer. A trial close is where you test the waters to see if your customer is ready to move forward.

It might sound like this: "Do you want to go with the red item or the blue one?"

Or, maybe: "Which of the two coaching programs seem like the best match for you?"

Your trial close can result in a sale or it may result in an objection.

When you gather enough information, you become clear about what people need and whether you can help them. When you do this, selling becomes easier because *you are serving.*

How to Anticipate and Overcome an Objection

Objections happen in the sales process all of the time. Don't take it personally.

When you do the first trial close, your customer will respond with a "yes" or a "no." If they respond with a "yes," great job! You just closed the sale effortlessly. However, when someone responds with a "no," there can be a number of reasons that they are not ready to move forward.

Here are some of the reasons they may give you:

- I can't afford it.
- I need to talk to my spouse.
- I haven't checked any other places yet.
- I need to think about it.

You may believe their objections and use them as an excuse for why your customer did not buy but are they REALLY true?

- When was the last time you went shopping for something you could not afford?
- When did you go shopping alone for something you needed your spouse's approval?

- When did you last tell someone that you wanted to shop around just to get out of making a decision?

Let's be honest.

What was the real reason you didn't buy?

What didn't the sales person do right?

Start paying attention to YOUR own behaviour as a customer. You can learn a lot from how sales people treat you and how it makes you feel.

What makes you buy and what stops you from doing business with certain sales people? Usually when a customer presents you with those objections it is because you have not offered them the right solution to their needs. That is typically the real reason why your customer is not ready to buy.

You can do two things when this happens—send them away to think about it, and a small percentage may come back, or do what a professional does and go back to determining their needs and ask some more questions to identify what you missed and see if you can find something that actually meets their needs.

When you take your time at building a rapport, determining your customer's needs, and you offer them the right solution, your closing rate will go way up. When you don't focus on building a rapport, you don't ask enough questions, and you offer the wrong solution, your closing rate will go way down.

Why is it that some people are able to easily sell and others constantly struggle? It's all in your ability to follow this simple process and to be confident while doing it.

Objections can often be overcome when you learn how to lean into them versus away from them. Anticipate common buying objections and, when someone says they cannot afford it, try leaning in and ask them what their budget is.

You will feel uncomfortable the first time you try and do this because it is normal for most people to just give up at the first no because we don't want to be "pushy."

If you really want to help your customer make a buying decision, however, you will do whatever you can to help him or her find the right solution and that means not avoiding the moment they say "no."

See objections as a normal part of the sales process and view them as a challenge to serve and offer a better solution to the customer. Take OWNERSHIP of the objection and identify how to overcome it.

If you are able to go back, gather more information, and overcome the objection, you may try closing on the same product/service again or you may offer something new depending on the information you have acquired.

How to Close the Sale

There are many ways to close the sale. Once you have determined needs, offered a solution, and overcome objections, you need to see if your customer is ready to buy.

This part of the sales process brings up all kinds of anxiety and is uncomfortable for many people because they are afraid of rejection. If you followed the steps I shared with you, you should experience rejection less often. And, if you remember what I discussed in Chapter Three about conversion rate, you should also expect a certain number of people not to buy.

Think of closing the sale as a natural part of the conversation. It's only awkward if you are. This is why following a system and even having a script that you use for how you close can be extremely useful while you are honing the skill. In The Sales Pilot, I go deeper into this and help people create scripts and systems to gain more comfort around selling.

Here is an example of what I might say when I am closing a sale (remember, this happens after all of the other steps above have taken place):

"Based on what you have shared with me, I would suggest my Quick Start Coaching Program. In this program, we take a detailed snapshot of where you are at in your business when we start, and we map out a plan to get you to where you want to be. It includes a strategy session where we create a roadmap for your success and is followed up by one coaching call each month for the next 5 months.

"What do you think? Would you like to do this work on your own or would you like my help?"

It's not a hard sell and most of the time people say to me, "Oh no, I can't do this on my own, I need your help." It's not pushy, but I am asking them to make a decision.

Notice in my close, I have summarized their needs again, I have shown how the program meets their needs, and I have asked them to make a decision.

If you are uncomfortable with a direct close like that, you may want to try a "which" close.

When you give your customer two options, it makes it easier for you to ask them which they prefer or which they would like to go with. For example, it could sound like, this: "Would you like to do the Quick Start Coaching program or would you prefer to join The Pilot Project?"

It is an assumptive close, meaning you are assuming that they are going to pick one of the two, but it gives them options and depending on which one that they gravitate towards you know the best way to serve.

Another way you can close the sale is if you get enough buying signals, you can be really direct and just ask how they would like to pay. Keep in mind when you are closing the sale and asking for money, this decision to buy is not about you. This decision is about them investing in themselves.

Let me explain what I mean.

You can buy a handbag at Walmart, Coach, or Louis Vuitton. All three fill the need of having a new bag. However, each comes with a distinctly different experience and price point.

I bought my first Louis Vuitton when I quit my job in 2006. I had coveted Louis Vuitton bags for years and had never bought one. I didn't buy one up until then because I wasn't ready to make that investment in myself.

It was the most money I had ever spent on a bag. In fact, it may have been the most expensive thing I had ever bought myself.

I was about to start a new chapter in my professional life, and I wanted this bag to represent this. There was a lot of emotion behind my decision. My objections in the store when I was trying to figure out which bag I wanted to buy had nothing to do with the sales rep. It had everything to do with me.

He had presented me with everything that I wanted in the most-effective manner you can imagine. I received the white-glove treatment. He was a master at selling luxury goods. I knew I wanted the Louis Vuitton bag. The only decisions were *how much* was I prepared to invest in myself and which bag was I going to choose?

The same is true when it comes to hiring a coach. You can hire a coach who charges $100 per hour, $1,000 per hour, or $100,000 per year. Learn to discern when you are uncovering needs exactly what your customer is looking for. The more clarity you have on what their needs, wants, and reasons for buying are, the easier it will be for you to close the sale.

When I finally found the bag I loved, the sales associate simply said, *"How would you like to pay for your new bag?"*

How to Add on Other Products or Services

When you become comfortable at upselling, you can increase the bottom line significantly in your business. Never assume that your client is only interested in one thing. You may be able to serve them in many ways.

In 2001, my husband and I built our first house. The contractor we worked with sent us out to buy light fixtures for installation by the electrician the next day. We had a detailed list of what we needed to buy for each room in the house, and off we went to Home Depot in search of our light fixtures.

When we were in the light department looking around at all of the different light fixtures, a Home Depot employee came and asked if he could assist us. We told him no, we were "just looking" and didn't need help. We continued to browse and filled two carts with light fixtures.

The Home Depot employee kept coming back to check on us and we kept telling him we did not need help. As we were walking out of the lighting department with our two shopping carts, he showed up one last time.

This time he said, *"Would you like help picking the correct light bulbs for each of those light fixtures?"*

This was an ah-ha moment and perfect opportunity to add on to our purchase because we were headed to the cash register, ready to pay, and go home. Light bulbs hadn't even crossed our minds because we were there to buy light fixtures.

Can you imagine how upset we would have been to get home only to realize we needed light bulbs, too?

The employee at Home Depot kept checking in even though we kept rejecting his offer to help. Then, at a key time when we really did need his help, he was there to add on to our purchase.

He did not take it personally each time we said "no." Instead he gave us space and kept coming back to check in because his orientation was to help us with our buying decision, not sell us.

Because of this, he was able to help us eventually by selling us some light bulbs, too.

Look for additional items that your customer might need when you are selling to them.

In my business, you can buy training programs, consulting and coaching services, or you can hire us to do the work for you. Some people start with a training program, then move into a coaching program, and eventually hire my team to do work for them. You, as a business owner, can strategically decide what options you want to offer to your customer in your business so that you always have the ability to add on.

How can you add something to your core product or service so that your customer has additional options when they are buying from you?

Start by making a list of all of the items you could add on, then survey some of your existing customers to see if there is any interest. You just may fill a need that your customers have that you didn't realize was there.

How Is Selling Online Different?

When you sell online, your copy has to do the work for you.

The sales copy you write builds trust and a rapport with the person who is on your website. You demonstrate in writing or through a video that you understand your customers' needs. You need to be able to show the benefits of your product or service, and most important, your copy must ask for the sale.

Writing good sales copy is hard to do and there are many ways to do this depending on what you are selling. The beautiful thing about social media and email marketing is when people have a relationship with you, your sales copy doesn't have to be quite as good as it does when you are trying to sell to a complete stranger.

I know this to be true because in my business often a simple email garners more business than a well-crafted sales page on my website.

A Final Note About Selling

A woman who works in the network marketing industry recently contacted me to see if I offered coaching programs to help people in her industry increase sales.

My response was this:

"Most of what I teach in my coaching programs is transferable from one business to the next. Having said that, I don't have specific expertise in the network marketing industry and, therefore, do not feel I am the best coach to serve your needs because there are other people out there who specialize in this industry. Can I refer you to a couple of people who might be able to help you instead?"

I don't want that individual to invest her money in working with me when I know I may not be able to serve her needs as well as someone else due to my lack of experience in her industry.

If you refer back to the chapter on defining your business model, you will recall that when you're really clear about what your business model is and what your product or service mix is, it's easy to stay true to that instead of saying "yes" to the things that don't fall into your model.

You don't walk into McDonald's to order sushi or the finest, freshest organic ingredients because you know McDonald's is fast food. McDonald's doesn't try to be a gourmet food brand because their business model is based on fast food delivery service.

Remember your business model and stay true to it, even when it's tempting to take on something that might generate a little bit of extra revenue.

That said, there are always exceptions.

Sometimes opportunities come up that you really want to participate in and suddenly those opportunities change the direction of your business.

When I first started my consulting business, I used to offer social media training, coaching programs, and strategy sessions. One day, one of my clients looked at me and said, "You're so good at this. Can't we just hire you to do it for us?" I thought about it and said, "Yes," I can do it and do it well—and now, because of that decision, I have an entire team who does social media community management for companies.

It's a natural fit with what I do but if someone asked me to manage the security department, it wouldn't make any sense, because that's not in alignment with what my core business is.

You have to ask yourself, *"Does this align with my core business model?"*

If it doesn't, chances are you're not going to be great at it and in that case you're just fragmenting your business focus. Nobody wants to buy from a generalist who is only *average* at what they do. People want to buy from people with a high level of expertise.

Make sure that when an opportunity shows up and you say "yes" that it's a real "yes" and that it's something you can really do well. Otherwise, you will end up in a situation you and your customers are not happy with.

If you choose to say "yes" to things not in alignment with your business model, you'll resent those clients and your business because you're settling. In essence, you're prostituting your business because you're taking money to do anything versus taking money to do something you're exceptional at.

Sell the right things to the right people at the right time.

Don't try to be all things to all people because unless you have a mass-market budget like Coca-Cola, you can't market to and be all things to all people. *You need to be able to focus your sales on the people who are the right fit for your business model.*

Practice Makes Perfect

In my 40s, I decided to learn how to swim. As an adult, this was one of the scariest things I ever decided to do. I had a tremendous fear of the water because I felt like I had no control and that I could drown if I ventured in too far.

My fear of water may feel similar to your fear of approaching and selling to a potential new customer.

In order to overcome this fear, I signed up for private adult swimming lessons and for several months, I went to the pool twice a week. During that time, I took baby steps into the water, practiced going out deeper, getting water on my face, going under water. Eventually, I was able to float, recover, and swim across the pool on my own.

That wouldn't have happened without regular practice and had I not taken lessons to learn the necessary skills to survive. You can't learn how to swim from the swim deck, and you can't learn how to sell without engaging with a potential customer.

Practice makes perfect. The only way to develop your skill is by putting theory into practice. Once you've practiced and developed the skill of selling, just like I was finally able to swim in the water, you will become more comfortable with selling and your closing rate will go up.

Practice and Evaluate Your Skill

No matter what business you are in, you need to practice your skills. The type of business you have will determine how often you'll be able to practice.

If you are located in a retail store, you can practice every day as long as someone comes into your establishment. If your business is consultancy based, you may need to do more things to get people involved in a discovery call with you, thus you may not be able to practice as much.

In order to assess your skill level, you need to find ways to evaluate how good you are at selling.

As a business coach, one of the things I do with my clients is to help them define the steps they're going to take to increase their sales because my ultimate goal is to help them increase sales and profits.

Many business owners operate on autopilot and never take the time to actually look at their performance and figure out what they are doing well or what they should change.

When I owned my retail store, I would teach my sales reps how to memorize the sales process we just went through and then I would listen to them go through it with potential customers.

Once the customer left the store, I'd ask them to self-assess on the different steps and they would offer the things they thought they did well and those they could have done differently or better.

We'd break down the interaction and discuss how they did with building a rapport, determining needs, paraphrasing, and overcoming objections with the closing the sale so that they could evaluate their skill in each area of the sales process. By doing this work together, they were able to learn which areas they excelled in and which areas they need to improve—or practice their skills in.

Each interaction that you have with a potential new customer may not have the exact same steps, but they should have a level of similarity if you are following a process.

If your interactions are radically different each time, you may have to ask yourself whether you're talking to the right potential customer. If you are attracting a wide and varied audience, chances are your messaging is not clear to your niche.

You should see some similarities in the people you're talking to. If there aren't any, your audience may be too varied, which is making it harder to convert sales.

The essential thing for you is to embrace the skill of selling.

Unless you are a grocery store clerk, you need to know how to sell and trust me even people in the grocery store business have a strategy around selling. They put things at eye level in a deliberate and intentional manner to drive sales through the placement of products. There is a strategy that goes into selling in a grocery store that just doesn't always involve the store clerk.

Many business owners are scared to sell. The thought of asking someone to buy makes them incredibly uncomfortable. Selling is a skill you can learn and I would argue it is one of the most important ones if you want to build a profitable and successful business.

Your business becomes a lot less vulnerable when you know how to sell. All of this is learnable, and just like I learned how to swim, I believe you can learn how to sell.

SECTION 5
CONCLUSION

CHAPTER ELEVEN

THE PILOT PROJECT

"The only action you will regret is the one you did not take."
– Suze Orman

I want to acknowledge you for getting to the last chapter of this book.

As you have read each chapter in this book you have gained insight into how to navigate modern entrepreneurship in your business.

I hope that you have also found many things to pilot in your own business in order to profit more. In many ways, this knowledge will arm you to be the pilot of your business, someone who is in control and ready to make your business fly higher than ever before.

You have learned about creativity; mindset; money; creating a business model; and how to create buckets, rocks, and distribution for your products and services. We have covered the importance of content creation for building credibility and why a community is so much more than an email list. You know the importance of email marketing, subject lines, and why your communication skills matter. We've identified why you don't need every social network out there and the power of relationship marketing. Last, you've learned a basic system for selling to your potential customers.

There is a possibility that you might be feeling overwhelmed with information and wondering what your next step should be.

Whether you are an aspiring entrepreneur who still has a day job but really wants to start a business or an existing business owner who craves change, challenge, and community, the next step you take matters and will put into motion all that subsequently happens.

You can choose to change the way you do business at any time. There is no change without some type of challenge and the greatest challenge is in deciding:

- Deciding that there is a different way to approach things. Then committing to the plan, one step at a time.
- Deciding you are worthy of following your dreams.

I am guessing that if you are like most people, you may not be dreaming big enough because it's scary. Remember, Chapter One *"The first sale is to yourself."*

You may feel very much alone on this journey. Many business owners share with me that they are the only one in their family who is self-employed and often don't know who to go to when they need support in their business.

There is a reason that people hire personal trainers, to get physically fit.

They know that when they work with a personal trainer, the trainer will push them harder than they will push themselves. However, there is usually a fork in the road that makes a person decide to hire a personal trainer.

It may be a health scare for you or someone in your family or it could be that you are tired of being tired and know that in order to change your life you first must change you.

The same decision process is true in business, too. Some people get stuck, others run out of money, and some are sick and tired of being sick and tired and not making any headway in their business.

You get to decide. You can decide to close this book like most people and continue with your business exactly the way things are, never making any changes. The struggle will be the same in spite of your newfound knowledge.

Alternatively, you can decide to do more and choose to make this your pilot and become part of a community of like-minded individuals who want to be guided further on how to take action on the principles shared in this book.

Your business is a marathon; it is not a sprint. It is a journey, and one that can last the better part of your lifetime.

If you are ready for change and you want to take the first step, I want to invite you to continue this journey with me in The Pilot Project.

The Pilot Project is not a test pilot. The Pilot Project is a proven system for business owners.

The Pilot Project is a program that hundreds of business owners just like you have taken to learn about the "business of business" and then used and applied that knowledge to move their business forward.

It is a program where YOU pilot the success of your business, on your terms. You navigate your own path, ensure that your business arrives at the destination you dream of with the least amount of turbulence, and generate the profits you want.

You become the captain of your business flight, and I am there to co-pilot and guide you along with the other co-pilots in this community.

It can be lonely being a business owner or aspiring entrepreneur, especially if your friends and family are not oriented towards business. You will find your "people" in The Pilot Project ready, willing, and able to share, support, encourage, and inspire you.

The Pilot Project is a program that is near and dear to my heart.

In many ways it was the inspiration for this book after seeing so many business owners struggle to make ends meet. I know there is an alternative way to run a business and where you can increase sales and profits and I would like to show you how.

One day, my intuition told me that I needed to share everything I do to build successful businesses in The Pilot Project.

The Pilot Project was designed to serve you in a big way. Most business programs like this cost thousands of dollars. This program, with complete access to get your questions answered along the way, is completely affordable.

One person told me this program was the straw that broke the camel's back and allowed her to close a million-dollar piece of business.

Building a business requires a lot of discipline, thought, and effort—especially if you are going to create a business that is profitable and stands the test of time.

There are many facets that go into making a business successful and throughout this book, I have tried to share with you the four cornerstones that I think are critical for your success.

Building a Solid Foundation Through Your Business Model

In the same way that you need a solid foundation when building a house, you require a solid foundation when creating your business model. Imagine if you built a home on a cracked or crumbling foundation. What would the outcome be?

The value of your home would decline and all that you had worked to create would be lost.

Think about your business the same way. The business model, processes, revenue streams, and distribution channels are all part of your foundation.

Creating Content That Builds Your Business Credibility

Content is not just a buzzword. Content is how people find you and your business through the Internet.

If your business does not have a content strategy for communicating with clients and leading clients to your doorstep, growing the business will be much harder than you expect it to be.

Knowing What and How to Sell

It isn't a business until you make a profit. If you are just trading four quarters for a dollar, you have a hobby not a business.

Selling is the most critical skill any business owner can have. Selling is a transfer of belief. You are selling your products and services to customers, and your ideas and passions to employees and vendors.

If you are not comfortable with selling, and the sales process, chances are you are leaving a lot of money on the table.

Knowing How to Utilize Social Media Marketing

It's easy to set up a page on Facebook today, but that is NOT the only thing you need to do when you build a business. You have to know what to do when a customer shows up or your business reputation will be at risk.

Each social network is different in how you connect with potential customers. You want to choose the right social networks for your business and know exactly how to use them if you expect social media to work for your business.

We have covered a lot in this book and you might be wondering, what is The Pilot Project and how can it help me? Allow me to tell you a bit more about it.

The Pilot Project

The first destination is your business foundation
This is perfect for business owners and aspiring entrepreneurs who want to go big. This phase of the program teaches the art of running *a business that makes money.* That's what makes it a business, right? Discover how to build a successful business model, measure your results and do more of what works, develop multiple revenue streams, and to communicate boundaries and set expectations with people, so that business relationships stay happy and profitable.

The second destination is your content
No more getting flustered by Facebook and Twitter or wondering what's the point of blogging. This phase of the program helps business owners master content marketing—quite simply, the technique of sharing your knowledge and opinions to grow an engaged audience of buyers. From now on, you'll always have something to say on social media, your business will be discovered by the right (paying) people, and you'll bring an aura of credibility to your products and services. You'll discover how to create content, build your list, then develop a deeper connection with that community through email marketing.

The third destination is increasing sales
What's *really* keeping you from making more money? This phase of the program teaches business owners how to get over their money hang-ups and how to sell, so that they can actually grow their business and keep some money in their pockets. If the thought of asking for money makes

you cringe or you think selling is sleazy, then this is for you. No one will ever care about your business as much as you do, and that means you have to be comfortable making a sale. Spoiler: you will be.

If you are ready to embark upon deeper learning and would like my support, I invite you to take the next step now. You can learn more about or join The Pilot Project the next time it takes off at **www. PilotToProfit.com/ThePilotProject**. You can also take advantage of a number of special bonuses when you join this community.

CHAPTER TWELVE
CONNECT WITH ME

"What women need now is to invest in themselves."
– Maria Shriver

I hope that we can continue this journey together whether The Pilot Project is for you or not. If the timing is not right for The Pilot Project, there are still tons of free resources for you to take advantage of at www.PilotToProfit.com/FreeTools.

You can gain access to additional reading material, my guide on setting up Facebook groups, free webinar replays, access recommended business podcasts and books that I personally use, a content plan for your business, plus other bonuses that I have set up specifically to help you.

Connections

To connect with me personally via email, please contact
Lisa@LisaLarter.com.

If you prefer to connect via social media, you will find my social
media links below:

www.Twitter.com/LisaLarter

www.Instagram.com/LisaLarter

www.Facebook.com/SocialMediaForYourBusiness

www.LinkedIn.com/in/LisaLarter

www.YouTube.com/LisaLarter

Free Training

If you would like to join my next live Profit Primer webinar, which
is designed to help business owners learn how to maximize sales and
profits for free, please visit www.LisaLarter.com/ProfitPrimer to register
your spot.

ABOUT THE AUTHOR

Lisa Larter, founder of The Lisa Larter Group, is a Business Consultant, Social Media Strategist, Author and Speaker. She works with businesses to maximize their profits and scale beyond their dreams, using social media, relationship marketing, and simple, eye-opening systems. She has helped increase the visibility and profits of a wide range of clients—including retail groups, authors, realtors, brick-and-mortar businesses, shopping centers, online entrepreneurs, and, her favorite big-name advisee, Deepak Chopra. His feedback? "Lisa, you're the best!"